Unbelievably Good Deals and Great Adventures That You Absolutely Can't Get Unless You're Over

50

Unbelievably Good Deals and Great Adventures That You Absolutely Can't Get Unless You're Over

50

Joan Rattner Heilman

CB

CONTEMPORARY BOOKS

Library of Congress Cataloging-in-Publication Data

Heilman, Joan Rattner.
    Unbelievably good deals and great adventures that you
absolutely can't get unless you're over 50 / Joan Rattner Heilman.
— 11th updated ed.
        p.   cm.
    Includes index.
    ISBN 0-8092-2792-4
    1. Travel.   2. Discounts for the aged.   I. Title.
G151.H44   1999
910′.2′02—dc21

99-24927
CIP

Cover design by Kim Bartko
Interior design by Terry Stone

Published by Contemporary Books
A division of NTC/Contemporary Publishing Group, Inc.
4255 West Touhy Avenue, Lincolnwood (Chicago), Illinois 60646-1975 U.S.A.
Printed in the United States of America
International Standard Book Number: 0-8092-2792-4
99 00 01 02 03 04 QP 18 17 16 15 14 13 12 11 10 9 8 7 6 5 4 3 2 1

Contents

Unbelievably Good Deals and Great Adventures That You Absolutely Can't Get Unless You're Over

50

1

Introduction to Good Deals and Great Adventures

This book is for people who love to do interesting things and go to new places—and don't mind saving money while they're at it. It is a guide to the perks, privileges, discounts, and special adventures to which you have become entitled simply because you've been around for 50 years or more.

On your 50th birthday (or on your 60th, 62nd, or 65th), you qualify for hundreds of special opportunities and money-saving offers that have lots of younger people wishing they were older—all for a couple of good reasons. First, as a person in your prime, you deserve them.

Second, as part of the fastest-growing segment of the American population, you represent an enormous market of potential consumers, a fact that has become quite apparent to the business community. More than a quarter of the U.S. population today is over 50; by 2020 that proportion is expected to increase to a third as the baby boomers turn 50 (one every 7.6 seconds). About 34 million Americans—1 in 8—are now over 65, and it is estimated that by 2030 this group will double. Besides, life expectancy is higher today than ever before (more than 61,000 Americans are 100 or older), and most of us can expect to live a long, healthy, and active life.

Those of us over 50 control most of the nation's wealth, including half of the discretionary income, the money that's left over after essentials have been taken care of, and almost 80 percent of its financial assets. Very often, the children have gone, the mortgage has been paid off, the house is fully furnished, the goal of leaving a large inheritance is not a major concern, and the freedom years have arrived at last.

As a group, we're markedly different from previous older generations who pinched pennies and saved them all. We, too, know the value of a dollar, but we feel freer to spend our money because we're better off than our predecessors, a significant number of us having accumulated enough resources to be reasonably secure. We also are far better educated than those before us, and we have developed many more interests and activities.

And, most important, we as a group are remarkably fit, healthy, and energetic. We are in *very* good shape—and feel that way. In fact, a survey has shown that most of us feel at least 15 years younger than our chronological age.

The business community is actively courting the mature market, as we are known, because now many of us have the time and the money to do all the things we've always put off. Because of the recognition of our numbers, our flexible schedules, and our vast buying power, we are finally being taken very seriously. To get our attention, we are increasingly presented with some real breaks and good deals, all detailed on these pages. We are also invited on trips and adventures specifically tailored to suit our interests, needs, and abilities.

In this book, you will learn how to get what's coming to you—the discounts and privileges you absolutely couldn't get if you were younger:

- Discounts at hotels and motels, at car-rental agencies, on buses, trains, and boats
- Price breaks on airfares from virtually all airlines
- Colleges and universities that offer you an education at bargain rates
- Insurance companies with discounts for people at 50 or thereabouts
- Travel adventures all over the world designed specifically for older travelers
- Clubs, trips, and services for mature singles
- Ski resorts where you can ski for half price—or for nothing
- Tennis tournaments, golf vacations, walking trips, bike tours, and senior softball leagues designed for you
- And much more!

Because every community has its own special perks to offer you, make a practice of *asking* if there are breaks to which you are entitled wherever you go, from movies to museums, concerts to historic sites, hotels to ski resorts, restaurants to riverboats, in this country and abroad. Don't expect clerks or ticket agents, tour operators, restaurant hosts, even travel agents to volunteer them to you. First of all, they may not think of it. Second, they may not realize you have reached the appropriate birthday. And third, they may not want to call attention to your age, just in case that's not something you would appreciate! You never know if you're being offered the best possible deal unless you ask. Many bargains and privileges are available only to people who speak up.

Remember to request your privileges *before* you pay or when you order or make reservations, and always carry proof of age or an over-50-club membership card, or, better yet, both. Sometimes the advantages come with membership in a senior club, but usually they are available to anyone over a specified age.

To make sure you're getting a legitimate discount when you want to take advantage of your over-50 privileges away from home, call the hotel, airline, car-rental company, or tour operator and ask what the regular or normal prices are. Find out if there's a special sale going on. Then decide whether you are getting a good deal. And, most important, always ask for *the lowest available rate* at the time you plan to travel and compare that with your discounted rate. Sometimes you'll find that even better specials are available.

With the help of this guidebook, completely revised and updated at least once a year, you will have a wonderful time and save money too.

2

Travel: Making Your Age Pay Off

People over 50 are the most ardent travelers of all. We travel more often, farther, more extravagantly, and for longer periods of time than anybody else. Ever since the travel industry discovered these facts, it's been after our business.

It's fallen in love with our age group because we have more discretionary income than people of other ages and more time to spend it. Besides, we are remarkably flexible. Many of us no longer have children in school, so we're free to travel at off-peak times or whenever we feel the need for a change of scenery. In fact, we much prefer spring and fall to summer. Some of us have retired, and others have such good jobs that we can make our own schedules. We can take advantage of midweek or weekend slack times when the industry is eager to fill space.

But, best of all, we are energetic, and we're not about to stay home too much. People over 50 account for about one-third of all domestic travel, air trips, hotel/motel nights, and trips to Europe and Africa. Nine out of ten of us are experienced travelers and savvy consumers.

Contrary to what a younger person might think, people in the mature generation aren't content with watching the action. Instead, we like to get right into the middle of it. There's not a place we won't go or an activity we won't try. Though many of us prefer escorted tours, almost half of us choose to travel independently.

Not only that, but we're shrewd—we look for the best deals to the best places. We are experienced comparison shoppers and seek the most for our money.

For all of these reasons, we are now offered astonishing numbers of travel-related discounts and reduced rates as well as special tour packages and other perks. Many agencies and tour operators have designed all or at least part of their trips to appeal to a mature clientele. Others include older travelers along with everyone else but offer us special privileges.

Most airlines sell senior coupon books, good for a year, that allow us to travel much more cheaply than other people or, instead, give those of us over 62 a 10 percent reduction on regular fares. And practically all hotel and motel chains—as well as many individual establishments—now offer similar inducements, such as discounts on rooms and restaurants.

There are so many good deals and great adventures available to you when you are on the move that we'll start right off with travel.

But, first, keep in mind:

■ Rates, trips, and privileges tend to change at a moment's notice, so check out each of them before you make your plans. Airlines and car-rental agencies are particularly capricious, and it's hard to tell what they offer from one week to the next. The good deals in this guidebook are those that are available as we go to press.

■ Always ask for your discount when you make your reservations or at the time of purchase, order, or check-in. If you wait until you're checking out or settling your bill, it may be too late.

■ Also remember that discounts may apply only between certain hours, on certain days of the week, or during specific seasons of the year. Research this before making reservations and always remind the clerk of the discount when you check in or pay your fare. Be flexible when you can and travel during the hours, days, or seasons when you can get the best deals.

■ It's particularly important when traveling to carry identification with proof of age or membership in a senior club. In most cases, a driver's license or passport does the job. So, in some cases, does the organization's membership card, a birth certificate, a resident alien card, or any other official document showing your date of birth. If you're old enough for a Medicare card or Senior ID card, use that.

■ Don't always spring for the senior discount without checking out other rates. Sometimes special promotional rates or discounts available to anybody any age turn out to be better deals. The car-rental companies and airlines, for example, are famous for this. Ask your travel agent or the ticket seller to figure out the *lowest possible available rate* for you at that moment.

■ Some of these bargains are yours at age 50, usually but not always tied to membership in a senior organization. Others come along a little later at varying birthdays, so watch for the cutoff points. Also, in most cases, if the person purchasing the ticket or trip is the right age, the rest of the party, a traveling companion, or the people sharing the room are entitled to the same reduced rates.

3

Out-of-the-Ordinary Escapades

If you are an intrepid, energetic, perhaps even courageous sort of person who's intrigued by adventures that don't tempt the traditional travelers, take a look at these unusual vacation suggestions, all of them planned specifically for the mature population. That means they usually offer you comfort and convenience even in the wild, and a leisurely pace with time for relaxation and independent exploration. Most important, they give you clean, comfortable accommodations—although perhaps a little rustic—and, whenever possible, a private bathroom. They are usually all-inclusive with most meals included. And they are certain to give you tales with which to entertain your friends, relatives, and acquaintances—at least until your next adventure.

ALASKA WILDLAND ADVENTURES

AWA's Senior Safaris are adventure tours for mature travelers who are looking for action and can move right along but want their comfort too. Several 10-day senior trips are offered in the summer, during which AWA also has similar but more ambitious ecotours for all ages. The itinerary, planned to accommodate all levels of ability and stamina, takes you down the Kenai River by raft then by yacht to watch whales, sea otters, glaciers, and birds; heading north, you tour national parks and view the wildlife.

Among other lodgings, your group stays at a wilderness lodge in Kenai Fjords National Park, and the Denali Backcountry Lodge in Denali National Park, with your own private bathroom. If you are a member of a recognized senior organization, you will get a $50 discount.

For information: Alaska Wildland Adventures, PO Box 389, Girdwood, AK 99587; 800-334-8730.

AMERICAN WILDERNESS EXPERIENCE

If you love adventurous vacations and roughing it in style, study the many offerings from AWE, an agency that's spent many years sending travelers on backcountry wilderness adventures and taking care of all the details. Its offerings are gathered from many tour operators and are open to all ages, but some are specifically designed for over-50s, and a few give discounts to seniors. Among these are a canoe trip in the Boundary Waters between Minnesota and Ontario, senior safaris in Alaska, horseback trips in Colorado or New Mexico, and a mountain sports week that combines rock climbing, horseback riding, mountain biking, and whitewater rafting in Colorado. Other trips feature special departures and itineraries for prime timers.

For information: American Wilderness Experience, PO Box 1486, Boulder, CO 80306; 800-444-0099 or 303-444-2622.

GREAT ALASKA SAFARIS

The Silver Safaris, scheduled several times a summer, were created expressly for older travelers who want comfort as well as adventure. Mellower than trips planned for all ages, the seven-day safaris start at the Great Alaska Fish Camp on the Kenai Peninsula, where you stay in riverside cabins and take a trip to Homer, a remote artists' community. After hikes and other adventures, plus a glacier-and-wildlife cruise in Prince William Sound and a visit to Anchorage, you fly to a wilderness camp in Lake Clark National Park to see bears, moose, and other creatures of the wild.

For information: Great Alaska Safaris, HC01, Box 218, Sterling, AK 99672; 800-544-2261.

HOSTELLING INTERNATIONAL/ AMERICAN YOUTH HOSTELS

This organization is probably best known for its low-cost bike and backpack trips for teenagers, but, in fact, it welcomes people of all ages. Once you become a member, you may participate in any of its "open" or "adult" adventures and book lodgings at the nearly 5,000 remarkably inexpensive HI hostels in more than 70 countries. Membership for adults costs $25 a year, but if you've reached the age of 55 you pay only $15. You will get a membership card, a guidebook listing 150 hostels in the United States and 80 in Canada, and access to all affiliated hostels worldwide.

The hostels vary from a castle in Germany to a lighthouse in California, a former dude ranch in Colorado, and a base camp in the Alps. Most hostels have kitchens where you prepare your own meals, and a few have cafeterias.

Members may stay at any hostel in the world, including the network of urban hostels located in Washington, D.C., New York, Boston, Pittsburgh, San Francisco, Seattle, Portland, Orlando, Miami Beach, New Orleans, Los Angeles, San Diego, and Honolulu. One night's stay costs $8 to $24. There is no maximum age limitation for booking a bed in these wonderfully cheap lodgings and hobnobbing with other hostelers who prefer not to pay exorbitant hotel prices. Be ready, however, to sleep in a double-decker cot in a sex-segregated dormitory for six or eight people supervised by "hostel parents." Many hostels have family or couple rooms, however, that can be reserved in advance.

For reservations at any of the 400 hostels around the world, members may call HI and, for a $5 fee, book accommodations in advance through its International Booking Network.

For information: HI/AYH, Dept. 855, 733 15th St. NW, Ste. 840, Washington, DC 20005; 202-783-6161.

HOSTELLING INTERNATIONAL–CANADA

A network of hostels throughout the Canadian provinces, HI-Canada offers members of all ages an inexpensive night's sleep in a wide variety of places ranging from modern facilities to historic homes, and refurbished jails to log cabins in the Rockies. Located in all major gateway cities and also in remote locations, your accommodations—private or shared—cost an average of $15 (Canadian) a night. Membership costs $25 (Canadian) per year and allows you to use any HI facility worldwide.

For information: Hostelling International–Canada, 205 Catherine St., Ste. 400, Ottawa, ON K2P 1C3; 800-663-5717 (Canada only) or 613-237-7884.

IMMERSIA TRAVEL

Catering only to adventurers over the age of 50, Immersia takes travelers to remote locales to explore local lifestyles and share other cultures in depth. Divided into three categories—easy, moderate, and vigorous—you may choose one that suits your abilities and tastes. The three-week tours include little-known areas of Bali; mountain villages in Turkey; Irian Jaya on the island of New Guinea; remote villages of Thailand; colonial Mexico; or the mountains of Nepal. You'll spend time with the local inhabitants and spend nights in native villages, immersing yourself in the culture. Before you go, you'll receive substantial resource packets about the places you will visit. On easy trips, you may travel by car, minivan, or leisurely walking and stay in local homes or guesthouses. On moderate adventures, add treks, trains, and four-wheel-drive vehicles with stays in village homes, cottages, and guesthouses. "Strenuous" may include travel in canoes, four-seater airplanes, and treks, while accommodations may be tents or village huts. Meals are always family style.

For information: Immersia Travel, 19 North King St., Leesburg, VA 20176; 800-207-5454 or 703-443-6939.

MT. ROBSON ADVENTURE HOLIDAYS

For people over 50 who crave action and the wilderness,

this agency plans a couple of "gentle adventures" every summer in British Columbia's Mt. Robson Provincial Park, just west of Jasper. Mt. Robson is the highest mountain in the Canadian Rockies, and the park offers spectacular scenery. The Fifty Plus Adventure is a five-night package trip for up to 14 participants that includes a guided trek, a nature tour, a marshlands canoe trip, and a gentle rafting float trip, all led by local naturalists. You sleep at the base camp in heated log cabins with private bathrooms and eat three hearty meals a day.

For information: Mt. Robson Adventure Holidays, PO Box 687, Valemount, BC V0E 2Z0; 250-566-4386.

OUTWARD BOUND

Outward Bound is famous for its rugged wilderness survival trips for young people aimed at building self-confidence, self-esteem, and the ability to work as a team. But it also offers short adventure courses specifically designed for adults, many for adults over the age of 50, who seek to examine their goals or gain personal insights. Among the recent one-week courses for these mature adventurers: a desert backpacking and canyon exploration trip in Big Bend National Park in Texas; rock climbing in the southern Appalachian Mountains of North Carolina; and whitewater rafting at Dinosaur National Park in Utah.

For information: Outward Bound, 100 Mystery Point Rd., Garrison, NY 10524; 888-882-6863 or 914-424-4000.

OVERSEAS ADVENTURE TRAVEL

OAT's soft adventures exclusively for travelers over 50 combine creature comforts with off-the-beaten-path experiences in exotic places all over the world, from the rain forests of Borneo to Botswana or the Galapagos Islands. Groups are small, with no more than 16 participants. The trips—rated from "easy" to "demanding"—move along at a leisurely pace and offer many optional side adventures. You'll travel by minivan and lodge in accommodations ranging from five-star hotels to jungle lodges, small inns, or spacious tents and sometimes use unconventional modes of transportation such as dugout canoes, camels, switchback trains, yachts, or your own two feet.

Among current tours, always including round-trip air, from this affiliate of Grand Circle Travel are excursions to such places as the Amazon, Peru, Morocco, Nepal, China, Tibet, Borneo, Kenya, and Europe.

Solo travelers are not charged a single supplement if they are willing to share accommodations, even if a room-mate has not been assigned.

For OAT's walking tours, see Chapter 13.

For information: Overseas Adventure Travel, 625 Mt. Auburn St., Cambridge, MA 02138; 800-873-5628.

RIVER ODYSSEYS WEST

ROW reserves a couple of whitewater river trips each summer exclusively for adventurous people over 55 who like to travel with others their own age. These Prime Time trips take you down Idaho's Salmon River and the Snake River on the Oregon border for five days, passing through four spectacular volcanic canyons. You travel in rubber rafts by day and sleep in tents at the edge of the river by night.

Another choice for mature travelers is one of ROW's

raft-supported walking trips in Hells Canyon or the Salmon River in Idaho. See Chapter 13 for details.

A third option for older travelers is a sea voyage in a motor-sail yacht along the southern coast of Turkey or along the coast of Croatia from Dubrovnik to Split.

For its canoe trips on the wild and scenic upper Missouri River in Montana, ROW reserves a couple of departure dates for adventurers over the age of 50. Following the trail of Lewis and Clark, you travel in comfortable 34-foot voyageur canoes carrying up to 14 passengers plus 2 guides. You'll float down the river for four or six days, stopping to explore many historic sites along the way. At the end of the day, you'll stop at luxury campsites with tents set up in advance, eat five-course meals, try your luck at fishing, and tell stories around the campfire.

For information: River Odysseys West, PO Box 579-UD, Coeur d'Alene, ID 83816; 800-451-6034 or 208-765-0841.

WARREN RIVER EXPEDITIONS

Warren River Expeditions offers many whitewater raft trips limited to adventurers over 50 plus two expeditions a year for grandparents and their grandchildren, taking them down Idaho's Salmon River, the longest undammed river in the country—fast and wild in the spring, tame and gentle in late summer. You'll float through unique ecosystems, down the deep Salmon River Canyon, and through the Frank Church Wilderness Area, where you'll view the lush scenery and abundant wildlife. Planned as soft adventure trips for people who are not enthusiastic about sleeping on the ground, the six-day senior trips limited to 16 guests put you up each night in comfortable rustic backcountry lodges. There's a 10 percent discount on all trips for those over 55 or under 16.

For information: Warren River Expeditions, PO Box 1375, Salmon, ID 83467-1375; 800-765-0421 or 208-756-6387.

INTERGENERATIONAL VACATIONS

Would you like to get to know your children or grandchildren better? Take them on vacation. A trip with the kids is a wonderful way to get close to them, especially for families who live many miles apart and seldom have a chance to get together. Whether it's a one-day tour of a nearby city or two weeks on a dude ranch, this is the kind of family togetherness that works. You can plan your own itineraries, maybe visiting places you both want to see, renting a cottage at the beach, or choosing a resort or cruise that offers special activities for the youngsters.

Or you can do it the easy way by deciding on a ready-made grandparent/grandchild vacation. Scheduled in the summer or during the usual winter school breaks, the best of the group tours are fully escorted by counselors, many of them schoolteachers on holiday. The tours, which range from a visit to Washington, D.C., to a safari in Kenya, go at a leisurely pace suitable to both generations with plenty of stops and time to relax and relate.

Growing in popularity too are other multigenerational holidays, such as adventures for mothers and grown daughters, hostelers and adult children, and whole families including children, parents, and grandparents. Here are some of the current choices for a vacation with the family.

AFC TOURS

Check out AFC's grandparent tours if you're looking for quality time with the children without the hassles of planning and traveling on your own. Scheduled during the summer holidays are trips to Yellowstone and Mt. Rushmore National Parks and visits to favorite U.S. cities, such as Boston and Washington, D.C. The supervised program includes activities for both age groups and a tour manager to lead the way. On each of these all-inclusive vacations, you'll stay in a first-class hotel with a swimming pool, only unpacking once per trip.

For information: AFC Tours, 11555 Sorrento Valley Rd., San Diego, CA 92121; 800-369-3693 or 619-481-8188.

ELDERHOSTEL INTERGENERATIONAL PROGRAMS

Elderhostel, whose basic programs are intended for people over 55, also offers many intergenerational programs. Some are for Elderhostelers and their children and/or grandchildren (or other young friends) under the age of 25; others are for hostelers and their adult children. Recent adventures in the U.S. have included, for example, a trip by wagon train in South Dakota, a study of wolves and their habitat in Minnesota, golfing in Texas, and a wildflower and geology exploration in the Rocky Mountains of Colorado. Current overseas programs include two-week adventures in Ireland, Scandinavia, or Greece.

For information: Elderhostel, 75 Federal St., Boston, MA 02110; 877-426-8056 (toll free) or 617-426-7788.

EXPLORATIONS IN TRAVEL

Multigenerational trips for mothers, daughters, grandchildren, aunts, and other female friends or relatives are scheduled at least once a year by Explorations in Travel, an agency specializing in active vacations for women over 40 (see Chapter 13). One current offering is a two-night windjammer cruise for landlubbers or experienced sailors aboard a 67-foot schooner in Penobscot Bay in Maine. On this adventure, one participant must be over 40 and the other under 21.

For information: Explorations in Travel, 1922 River Rd., Guilford, VT 05301; 802-257-0152.

FAMILYHOSTEL

Learning adventures in foreign countries are the specialty of FamilyHostel, a program sponsored by the University of New Hampshire Division of Continuing Education, but more domestic vacations have been added. It takes families—perhaps you and your school-age grandchildren—on 10-day all-inclusive vacations in the summer to such places as France, Switzerland, Austria, Wales, Italy, Mexico, and Costa Rica. Some of the trips are exclusively for grandparents or parents over the age of 50 and children 8 to 15 years old.

Separately and together, you'll enjoy workshops, recreation, sight-seeing, and social events including interaction with the local people. The groups are accompanied by a university representative and teachers from the U.S. and the host country. There is lodging in hotels, university residence halls, or apartments, and the cost is moderate for what you get.

In 1999, FamilyHostel adds family vacations in the U.S.; its first trip is based at the university with excursions to other parts of New England.

For information: FamilyHostel, University of New Hampshire, 6 Garrison Ave., Durham, NH 03824; 800-733-9753 or 603-862-1147.

GRANDEXPLORERS

The twice-a-year, 10-day tours of Israel from GrandExplorers, a program created by B'nai B'rith, are designed to help grandparents pass along Jewish family heritage, values, and traditions to the younger generation. Included are stays in Jerusalem and Tel Aviv, a jeep tour of the Golan Heights, a camping trip with a Bedouin family for the children, camel rides, visits to historic sites throughout Israel, and two nights on a kibbutz.

For information: GrandExplorers, B'nai B'rith Center for Jewish Identity, 1640 Rhode Island Ave. NW, Washington, DC 20036; 800-500-6533 or 202-857-6577.

GRANDPARENTS' HOUSEPARTY

Choose from among more than 10,000 private homes—from cottages to castles—in England, Ireland, Scotland, or Wales, and take the kids along for a week or more. Country Cottages offers its Grandparents' Houseparty package that at some times of the year costs about $100 a day per person, including round-trip air from New York and a rental car or minivan, and in some seasons adds a small discount for grandparents and grandchildren. All of the properties are second homes equipped with linens, tableware, and cookware and have accessible caretakers to provide information or assistance.

For information: Country Cottages, Box 810997, Boca Raton, FL 33481-0997; 800-674-8883.

GRANDTRAVEL

Grandtravel pioneered the notion of taking grandparents and their grandchildren on vacation together. Its 2 trips a year have grown to over 20. For grandparents of any age and children aged 7 to 17, its tours include visits to Southwest Indian country, Alaska, or Scandinavia; barge trips in Alsace and Holland; tours of famous castles in England and Scotland; and safaris in Kenya. If you want to go on your own, the agency will also arrange a special tour just for your family group. You needn't be an authentic grandparent, either—aunts, uncles, cousins, godparents, and other surrogate grandparents are welcome.

Tours, each designated for certain ages of children, are led by teacher-escorts, range from 7 to 18 days, and always include plenty of rest stops and time for both generations to spend time alone with their own age groups. As part of its package, Grandtravel provides predeparture counseling to help you deal with any special concerns such as what to pack or how to deal with kids who miss their moms.

For information: Grandtravel, The Ticket Counter, 6900 Wisconsin Ave., Chevy Chase, MD 20815; 800-247-7651 or 301-986-0790.

GREAT CAMP SAGAMORE

Take your grandchild to camp with you for a week in the summer. The site is the Great Camp Sagamore, a former Vanderbilt wilderness retreat in New York State's Adirondack Park, and the purpose is to bring the two generations together to have fun and get to know one another better.

Mornings, the campers engage in joint activities such as walks, berry picking, games, and nature art. Afternoons, the age groups are on their own, free to choose from options that include music, crafts, and swimming. Before dinner, grandparents meet for discussions of their own issues, and in the evenings everyone gets together for stories, campfires, sing-alongs, square dancing, and other activities.

For information: Great Camp Sagamore, PO Box 146, Raquette Lake, NY 13436; 315-354-5311.

IRISH FESTIVAL TOURS

For a visit to your Irish roots, gather up your grandchildren (or nieces, nephews, or other young friends) this summer and take them on a 10-day tour that includes Dublin, Avoca, Waterford, Killarney, the Ring of Kerry, and Galway. You'll learn about the folklore and traditions of the Irish people; visit castles, villages, farms, and museums; listen to storytellers; go pony trekking; see a working dairy farm; learn traditional dances; and otherwise enjoy a respite just for you and the grandkids. Most activities include both generations, but some separate events are planned as well.

For information: Irish Festival Tours, PO Box 169, Warminster, PA 18974; 800-441-4277.

RASCALS IN PARADISE

Specializing in family vacations for parents and children, Rascals in Paradise also invites grandparents and grandchildren to go along on its adventure trips to such places as Mexico and the Caribbean, the Bahamas, Europe, New

Zealand, Thailand, Australia, the Canadian Rockies, Africa, the Galapagos Islands, Hawaii, Alaska, and ranches in the West. All group trips, three to six families per group, include escorts who plan activities for the older children and arrange baby-sitters for the little ones. This agency will plan independent vacations, too, as well as family reunions and other multigenerational celebrations.

For information: Rascals in Paradise, 650 Fifth St., Ste. 505, San Francisco, CA 94107; 800-872-7225 or 415-978-9800.

ROOTS & WINGS EXCURSIONS

Intergenerational travel is the specialty here. Among other family-oriented excursions, many trips are planned exclusively for grandparents and their grandchildren, and more just for mothers and their adult daughters. The GrandTrips include weekend adventures with other grandfamilies to such places as the Florida Keys, the Florida space coast, Amish country, and Civil War battlefields. Longer domestic journeys currently go to Hawaii, the Canadian Rockies, the Wild West, Alaska, and Chesapeake Bay. Abroad, destinations include the British Isles and Italy. Weekend excursions for mothers, daughters, and grandmothers include Charleston, San Francisco, Scottsdale, and Sedona.

For information: Roots & Wings Excursions, 11025 Howland Dr., Reston, VA 20191; 800-722-9005 or 703-391-9639.

SIERRA CLUB

A remarkably inexpensive summertime vacation for grandparents and their grandchildren led by experienced volunteers is on the list of the Sierra Club's famous outings. A laid-back and relaxed holiday, it's a six-day stay at the Sierra Club's own rustic lodge near Donner Pass, in California's Sierra Nevadas. The outing is designed for people between 5 and 95, and all activities are optional. You lodge in rather spartan rooms, eat hearty meals, and enjoy yourselves doing such things as hiking, strolling, climbing to the top of Donner Peak, taking the tram to the top of Squaw Valley, having a picnic at Donner Lake, fishing, swimming, visiting historic sites, and singing around the campfire.

For information: Sierra Club Outing Dept., 85 Second St., San Francisco, CA 94105; 415-977-5522.

VISTA TOURS

The family tours offered by Vista are designed for children and their relatives, whether grandparents, parents, aunts and uncles, or otherwise. There are several different trips, ranging from 4 to 14 days, such as the Railroads of the Rockies, Southern California Art and Studio Tour, the Idaho and Oregon Trial, and the California National Parks. Activities are planned for the different generations separately and together.

For information: Vista Tours, 1923 N. Carson St., Ste. 105, Carson City, NV 89701; 800-248-4782.

WARREN RIVER EXPEDITIONS

Take the grandkids down the Salmon River in Idaho on a raft trip run by Warren River Expeditions. You'll sleep in comfortable backcountry lodges, some quite rustic, along the river's edge and have plenty of exciting adventures on the big rubber rafts powered by expert oarspeople. At least two midsummer departures, with a 10 percent discount for those over 55 or under 16, are reserved each summer for the two generations.

For information: Warren River Expeditions, PO Box 1375, Salmon, ID 83467-1375; 800-765-0421 or 208-756-6387.

4

Cutting Your Costs Abroad

The most enthusiastic voyagers of all age groups, Americans over 50—one out of three adults and a quarter of the total population—spend more time and money on travel than anybody else, especially when it comes to going abroad. It's been estimated that more than 4 out of every 10 passport holders are at least 55 years old. And there's hardly a country in the world today that doesn't actively encourage mature travelers to come for a visit, because everybody has discovered that they are travel's biggest potential market.

Because you are now being avidly pursued, you can take advantage of many good deals in other lands. Airlines, for example, often give you fare reductions on domestic flights within the country. Railroad and bus systems in most European countries offer deep discounts to seniors that are especially valuable if you plan an extended stay in one place. Even ferries and cruise ships are often ready to make you a deal. This chapter gives you a rundown on these and other ways to cut your European holiday costs, especially if you are planning your trip on your own. For the U.S. and Canada, see Chapter 9.

But, first, keep in mind:

■ Always ask about senior savings when you travel on trains, buses, or boats anywhere in the world. Do the same when you buy tickets for movies, theater, museums, tours, sight-seeing sites, historic buildings, and attractions. Don't assume, simply because you haven't heard about them or the ticket agent hasn't mentioned them, that they don't exist. They are becoming more and more common everywhere and you'll be amazed how much money you can save.

■ Some countries require that you purchase a senior card to take advantage of senior discounts, but most require only proof of age, usually in the form of a passport.

■ Always have the necessary identification with you and be ready to show it. Occasionally you may need an extra passport photograph.

■ For specifics on a country's senior discounts, call its national tourist office.

■ Call Rail Europe (800-438-7245), which represents most European railways, for information about train passes.

■ Your passport may be required along with your rail pass while you are in transit, so keep it with you.

■ Rail passes, including many national passes, sold in the U.S. and Canada can be bought from any travel agency or directly from Rail Europe. The national passes are often available only at major rail stations or airports within a country. Be prepared to show your passport.

■ Major U.S. hotel chains, such as Radisson, Marriott, Hilton, Holiday Inn, and Best Western, offer senior discounts that almost always apply at their participating properties in other countries.

■ Travel passes for sight-seeing are available in confusing profusion, and, since many overlap and some must be purchased before you leave home, it's wise to check them out before you go by contacting the national tourist offices of the countries you plan to visit.

■ Tourist passes usually cost older travelers the same as everyone else, but in most cases they are definitely worth buying. Among the best buys everywhere are the inexpensive, easy-to-use "city cards" available for many major European cities. Usually good for one to four days, they give you free public transportation plus admission to the most important tourist sites. Many also offer discounts on tours, meals, theater tickets, cultural attractions, and shopping.

EUROPE BY RAIL

Rail passes make the going cheaper in Europe, especially if you travel with a companion or a group, and it's easier to use them than to buy tickets as you go. Besides, some of them offer senior discounts. It's not a simple matter to sort them all out, however. Some are multinational, good for travel in more than one country. Others are valid only within the borders of one country; these are usually designed for residents but can be useful to tourists as well.

Most passes are available in two different versions: a flexi-pass that permits travel for a specified number of days within a certain time period, and a consecutive-day pass that is valid on any day within a certain period. Many are not available overseas and must be purchased on this side of the Atlantic before you go. Others may only be purchased in the country that issues them.

FINDING A DOCTOR OVERSEAS

Before you leave on a trip to foreign lands, it would be wise to send for IAMAT's list of physicians all over the world who speak English or French, have had medical training in Great Britain, the U.S., or Canada, and have agreed to reasonable preset fees. When you join the free nonprofit **International Association for Medical Assistance to Travellers** (IAMAT), you will get a membership card entitling you to services and its prearranged rates, a directory of physicians in 125 countries and territories, a clinical record to take along with you, and advice on immunizations and preventive measures. Information about climate, food, water, and sanitary conditions in 1,450 cities is given to members who donate $25 or more.
For information: IAMAT, 417 Center St., Lewiston, NY 14092; 716-754-4883.

EURAILPASS AND EUROPASS

The Eurailpass gives you free unlimited first-class train travel in Hungary and on all the major railways of Western Europe except those in Great Britain. There is no senior discount on this pass, but it is worth considering if you plan to cover many miles in many countries. On the other hand, if you are visiting just one country, you'd probably do better with that nation's senior discounts or national pass. Available for various numbers of days up to three months, the Eurailpass also entitles you to free or discounted travel on many buses, ferries, steamers, and suburban trains. If you are traveling with at least one other person, you can get a Eurail Saverpass or Eurail Saver Flexipass, which is an even better deal.

The Europass, less expensive, is another option. It is good for unlimited first-class train travel any time within a two-month period in five western European countries (France, Germany, Italy, Spain, and Switzerland). Other countries may be added with a surcharge.

None of these passes is sold in Europe—they must be purchased before you leave home. And none gives seniors a special break.

For information: Rail Europe, 2100 Central Ave., Boulder, CO 80301; 800-4-EURAIL (800-438-7245).

SCANRAIL SENIOR PASS

Sold only on this side of the Atlantic, the Scanrail Pass gives you unlimited travel in Denmark, Finland, Norway, and Sweden. If you're over 60, buy the Scanrail Senior Pass. It offers you the same privileges, but for about 10 percent less than younger adults pay. For details, see "Scandinavia" later in this chapter.

For information: Rail Europe, 2100 Central Ave., Boulder, CO 80301; 800-4-EURAIL (800-438-7245).

EUROSTAR: THE CHANNEL TUNNEL

Eurostar offers 12 round-trips a day through the tunnel that goes under the English Channel connecting Paris or Brussels with London. The senior fares—you're eligible if you're over 60—are about 27 percent less than the regular adult fares on first-class tickets. They are also unrestricted and refundable.

For information: Rail Europe, 800-EUROSTAR or 800-4-EURAIL (800-438-7245).

COUNTRY-BY-COUNTRY TRAVEL DEALS

AUSTRIA

If you are a woman over 60 or a man over 65, you may travel around Austria at half fare if you first buy an official Senior Citizen Railway Card from the railroad for about $30. Buy it at major rail stations in Austria or Germany or get one by mail from Austria. It allows travel on the Austrian Federal Railways, the bus system of the Federal Railways, and the Postal Service.

And be sure to look into the Vienna Card and similar discount cards in other cities and provinces in Austria, including Salzburg, Linz, and Innsbruck. These cards get you free public transit plus free or reduced admissions to the most important tourist attractions.

For information: Austrian National Tourist Office, PO Box 1142, New York, NY 10108; 212-944-6880.

BELGIUM

The Golden Railpass for travelers, domestic or foreign, over the age of 60 allows six single-rail journeys between any two stations in Belgium at a cost that is currently 1,260 Belgian francs (about $7.25) for second class and 1,940 francs (about $11) for first class. The pass is also valid for a traveling companion over 55 or under 12. Buy it at any railroad station.

If, however, you plan to use the train regularly, a better choice may be the Half-Fare Card that is available to travelers of any age. It gives you 50 percent off the fare, first or second class, on all journeys within a month. Current cost: 600 francs (about $3.50).

At 62, you are entitled to a 10 percent discount on most fares when you fly Sabena from here to Europe.

Something else to remember: Most hotels in Brussels offer a 50 percent reduction on room rates on weekends and during the months of July and August when the staffs of many international organizations leave town for home.

For information: Belgian National Tourist Office, 780 Third Ave., New York, NY 10017; 212-758-8130.

BERMUDA

February is Golden Rendezvous Month in Bermuda, when visitors over the age of 50 are treated to special events and free activities every day. For example, there are complimentary bus tours around the island, and talks on the traditions, culture, history, flowers, and wildlife. Plus, there are bridge tournaments, ballroom dancing, and visits to museums. Many hotels offer special packages and rates, while the Visitors' Service Bureau distributes two free ferry/bus tokens per person as well as discount coupon books to use at retail stores and sight-seeing attractions.

For information: Bermuda Department of Tourism, 205 E. 42 St., New York, NY 10017; 800-223-6106.

DENMARK

In this charming country, visitors over the age of 65 get a 50 percent discount on the Danish State Railway every day except Friday and Sunday, when they get 20 percent off. Buy your tickets at any train station and be prepared to prove your age.

Ask for your senior discount of 10 percent when you fly SAS from North America to Europe. And remember that at age 65 SAS will also take 20 percent off certain fares, depending on the route, for domestic flights within Denmark.

And don't forget to buy the Copenhagen Card. Available for 24, 48, or 72 hours, it provides free unlimited travel by bus and train throughout the metropolitan region; free admission to more than 60 museums and historic sites; and discounts on car rentals, canal rides, and ferry crossings. City cards are also sold for Odense and Aalborg.

For information: Danish Tourist Board, 355 Third Ave., New York, NY 10017; 212-885-9700.

FINLAND

If you are over 65, you need only to show some ID such as your passport at the ticket office to get half fare on trains and a 30 percent reduction on bus journeys at least 80 kilometers long.

What's more, you'll get 10 percent off transatlantic flights on Finnair and a whopping 70 percent off the normal fare on domestic flights on Finnair and Air Bothnia. You must show identification and pay for your tickets within three days of booking your flight. Changes require a small charge.

And don't forget to pick up the Helsinki Card at a

tourist office, your hotel, or the airport. It's good for more than 50 discounts at places you'll want to visit.

For information: Finnish Tourist Board, 655 Fifth Avenue, New York, NY 10017; 212-885-9700.

FRANCE

Visitors as well as residents over 60 are entitled to discounts on the French National Railroad (SNCF). The Decouverte Senior rate, designed for infrequent travelers, is yours simply by showing ID when you buy your ticket in the station. It gives you a 25 percent discount on the standard fares.

The Carte Senior rate, for frequent travelers, is valid for a year and gives you unlimited travel at reduced rates—50 percent discount on a limited number of seats for some journeys during non-rush hours and a 25 percent discount on others. The card currently costs about $47 and requires a passport photo when you buy it at any major train station. It also gives you a 30 percent reduction on standard fares on train trips to 23 other European countries.

Always ask for a senior discount, again offered at age 60, wherever you go in France, from museums to historic sites, movies, concerts, and cultural attractions. And remember to get your 10 percent discount on Air France flights to Europe.

For information: French Government Tourist Office, 444 Madison Ave., New York, NY 10022; 212-838-7800.

GERMANY

Many restaurants in Germany offer a *Seniorenteller,* a special menu that offers lighter fare in smaller portions at less cost for older guests. Ask to see it. Also ask if there are discounts for seniors everywhere else you go—you will find they are available in such places as department stores, hair salons, and, of course, museums and tourist sites. Even some hotels and spa resorts have them, especially during off-peak seasons.

There is a 10 percent discount on most fares across the Atlantic Ocean to European destinations on Lufthansa for people 60 and older. The same discount applies to domestic flights within Germany.

Finally, check out the city cards, now available at local tourist offices in Berlin, Hamburg, Frankfort, Munich, Dresden, and Weimar.

For information: German National Tourist Office, 122 E. 42 St., New York, NY 10168; 212-661-7200.

GREAT BRITAIN

Bargains abound in the U.K., where senior discounts and special rates apply almost everywhere from railroads and bus lines to museums, theaters, and historic sites. Be sure to ask wherever you go if there is an OAP (Old Age Pensioners) rate.

For information: British Tourist Authority, 551 Fifth Ave., New York, NY 10176; 800-GO 2 BRIT (800-462-2748) or 212-986-2200.

Traveling by train: In Britain, where virtually every town may be reached by train, it pays to consider a rail pass, especially since travelers over 60 get discounts of 10 to 15 percent off the regular adult prices.

The BritRail Senior Flexipass, for example, allows 4-, 8-, or 15-day unlimited first-class travel within a month in England, Scotland, and Wales. The BritRail Senior Classic

Pass, again for unlimited first-class travel, is good for 8, 15, 22, or 30 consecutive days. If you are traveling in a group, the third and fourth persons in your party receive an additional 50 percent off either of the senior passes.

If you are traveling with children, your senior pass (or an adult card) allows one accompanying child 5 to 15 years old to travel free; additional children 5 to 15 years of age go at half-price; children under 5 are always free.

These passes are not sold in Britain but must be purchased before you leave this side of the Atlantic. They are not accepted in Ireland or on special excursion trains. With all passes, you may get on and off the trains as often as you like along the way.

Travel passes: Many cost-saving passes are available for seeing the sights in Britain.

Don't leave home, for example, without a Great British Heritage Pass for unlimited free entry to hundreds of castles, abbeys, palaces, manor homes, museums, and gardens in England, Scotland, Wales, and Northern Ireland. Buy it from BritRail or Rail Europe before you leave, or from Tourist Information Centres in Britain. A seven-day pass currently costs about $45.

The London Visitor Travelcard gives you unlimited travel for 3, 4, or 7 consecutive days on London's buses and subways as well as many trains in the London area. It includes transfer via underground from Heathrow Airport to central London.

For information: BritRail, 888-BRITRAIL (888-274-8724); in Canada, 800-555-BRIT (800-555-2748); or Rail Europe, 800-4-EURAIL (800-438-7245).

Northern Ireland: Seniors pay half price for a Freedom of Northern Ireland Ticket, issued for 1 or 7 days, that gives free access to all services of Citybus, Northern Ireland Railways, and Ulsterbus. Buy the pass at railway stations.

Scotland: Sixty historic attractions, from castles to abbeys and distilleries, are yours to see when you purchase a Scottish Explorer Ticket for 7 or 14 days. Ask for your senior discount when you purchase it at a Historic Scotland property or a Tourist Information Centre in Scotland.

CHECK OUT YOUR HEALTH INSURANCE

When you travel to foreign countries, remember that Medicare does not provide coverage for health-care services outside of the U.S.—except in Canada and Mexico. So if you do not have private health insurance that will pay these expenses if you incur them overseas, talk to your travel agent about purchasing temporary insurance that covers you for the length of your trip. Some policies cover trip cancellation/interruption and lost baggage as well.

Discount cards: In London, Bath, York, and Edinburgh, discount cards—London for Less, Bath for Less, York for Less, and Edinburgh for Less—may be purchased at Tourist Information Centres in those cities. They give you discounts at museums, attractions, concerts, tours, restaurants, shops, and more.

Traveling by bus: If you plan to travel extensively by bus, consider buying a Tourist Trail Pass that discounts fares on National Express and Scottish Citylink Services. It gives you unlimited travel throughout England, Scotland, and Wales for varying numbers of consecutive days and costs you, if you are over 50, about 25 percent less than it

does younger adults. You must buy the pass in the U.S.
For information: British Travel International, PO Box 299, Elkton, VA 22827; 540-298-1395.

GREECE

Here, if you are at least 60, you may buy a rail pass, valid for a year, at any major railroad station in Greece and use it for five complimentary train trips anywhere you want to travel in the country off-season (October 1 to June 30). It is not good on the 10 days before or after Easter or Christmas. When the five free trips have been used, the pass provides you with a 50 percent discount on rail tickets. Current cost for the pass is approximately $55 for first class.

On domestic air travel, Olympic Airways makes big reductions in fares for passengers over 60.
For information: Greek National Tourist Organization, 645 Fifth Ave., New York, NY 10022; 212-421-5777.

IRELAND

Many hotels in the Republic of Ireland offer senior discounts, especially off-peak, so make it a policy to inquire about them when making your reservations. In most cases, you must be 65 to qualify. Theaters (midweek), national monuments, and historic sites give you price reductions too. Always ask. Also one tour company, CIE Tours International (800-CIE-TOUR), gives a discount of $55 on a few of its coach tours to the first fifteen people over 55 who sign up.

No doubt you'll be spending time in Dublin, so it would be wise to buy a Dublin Supersaver Card, which reduces the admission fees by up to 30 percent for a group

of museums, castles, and attractions. Good for a year, it currently costs 16 pounds (about $25) for an adult pass, but
if you are an OAP (Old Age Pensioner, for which you qualify at 60 or 65) you'll get it for 12½ pounds (about $20).
It is available at Dublin Tourism Information Centres
around the city.
For information: Irish Tourist Board, 345 Park Ave., New
York, NY 10154; 800-223-6470 or 212-418-0800.

ITALY

The Carta d'Argenta (Silver Card), which currently costs
about $25 and is valid for a year, entitles anyone over 60,
tourist or resident, to a 20 percent discount on all rail
travel in Italy. You buy it at railroad stations in Italy at the
special windows (Biglietti Speciali) and, to get the lower
fares, show it when you buy your tickets. It is not available
on this side of the Atlantic. This card will obviously save
you money if you plan to travel extensively in Italy, but the
Flexi-Rail Pass or Italian Railcard, available to persons of
any age, which may only be purchased in the U.S. for 4 to
30 days of unlimited travel within a month, may prove to
be a better value for shorter stays with less mileage. Check
out all of your choices before making a decision.

Remember also to request your senior discount of 10
percent when you fly Alitalia across the ocean. To get it, you
must be 62. At 65, request the discounted Terza Era fares.
For information: Italian Tourist Board, 530 Fifth Ave., New
York, NY 10111; 212-245-4822.

JAPAN

More than 25 museums and art galleries in and around
Tokyo now offer free or discounted admission to travelers

65 or older who show identification such as a passport. Also available in Japan are free Welcome Cards that allow discounts on hotels, restaurants, recreation facilities, shopping, and cultural attractions in four regions of the country. Pick them up at official tourist information centers. With these cards, you'll get a local guidebook and often an area map.

And more: Goodwill Guides System (SGG) connects you with local citizens in 27 cities in Japan who are ready to give you free tours.

For information: Japan National Tourist Organization, 1 Rockefeller Plaza, New York, NY 10020; 212-757-5640.

LUXEMBOURG

Although this small country offers no special advantages to visitors over 50 on its transportation system, its Rail Network tickets, available to everyone for varying lengths of time and distances on railways and public buses, are cheap and efficient. For example, you may buy a booklet of 10 short-distance tickets for 320 francs (about $9) or a one-day network ticket for 160 francs (about $5).

The LuxembourgCard, also for everyone, is another good investment for sightseers, giving free public transportation; free access to museums, castles, historic sites, and cultural attractions; plus discounts on sight-seeing tours.

For information: Luxembourg National Tourist Office, 17 Beekman Pl., New York, NY 10022; 212-935-8888.

NETHERLANDS

Whenever you go to museums, attractions, cultural and historic sites, or on tours in Holland, always ask if there is a senior discount because people over 65 are usually given a break on admission fees. Have your passport handy to prove your age.

If you plan to travel around the country, it may make sense to buy a Holland Railpass, which must be purchased from Rail Europe (800-4-EURAIL) before you go because it is not available in the Netherlands. Travelers over 60 years of age get a substantial discount on passes good for three or five days. The current cost for seniors for three days is $119 first class or $79 second class. Other passes, without senior discounts, are also available.

At 65, you may buy a "strippenkart," good for 15 rides on buses, metros, and trams throughout Holland, for about $3.25 or half the regular adult price. Get it at railway stations, shops, or post offices.

And consider the Amsterdam Culture & Leisure Pass (about $18 for all adults). It provides vouchers for free or discounted admission to museums, cruises, tours, and more.

On flights within Europe from Amsterdam, you can get a 10 percent discount at age 60.

For information: Netherlands Board of Tourism, 225 N. Michigan Ave., Chicago IL 60601; 888-GO-HOLLAND (888-464-6552).

NEW ZEALAND

Travelers over 60 are entitled to a Golden Age discount of 30 percent off the standard adult fares booked in New Zealand on all Tranz Scenic Trains any time of year. Buy your tickets at a railroad station or a visitor information office in New Zealand.

In addition, the 50+ Club at CLD Hotels—Millennium,

Copthorne, and Quality—throughout the country offers you a 30 percent discount when rooms are available.

And don't forget: Whenever you go to New Zealand, ask if there is a senior discount for which you qualify.

For information: New Zealand Tourism Board, 501 Santa Monica Blvd., Santa Monica, CA 90401; 800-388-5494 or 310-395-7480.

NORWAY

In this beautiful country, you're entitled to half fare on buses and railways, first or second class, any time, any place. For this break, however, women must be at least 65 and men 67 and ready to prove their age with a proper ID.

At age 60, you become eligible for a discount on many Color Line cruises, and at age 67 on Norwegian Coastal Voyages (except from June 1 to July 15). (See "Bergen Line" in Chapter 5.)

SAS, the Scandinavian airline, not only offers passengers over 62 a 10 percent discount on flights between North America and Europe, but also gives those over 65 special senior fares on domestic flights within Norway on tickets sold in the U.S. At age 67, passengers are entitled to a 50 percent discount on domestic flights within Norway when tickets are purchased in that country.

As for hotels, there are discounts for all of Scandinavia (discussed later in this chapter). In addition, check out the Norway Fjord Pass, which costs about $10 and offers discounts on rooms from May through September in hotels, guest houses, apartments, and holiday cottages.

As you should everywhere, consider purchasing city cards, which in Norway include the Oslo Card and the

Bergen Card. They will provide free public transportation plus free or discounted admission at most museums, historic sites, and cultural attractions.

For information: Norwegian Tourist Board, 655 Fifth Ave., New York, NY 10017; 212-885-9700.

PORTUGAL

If you're over 65, there's hardly anywhere you can go in Portugal without being offered a senior discount of 30 to 50 percent off the regular price. So make a point of asking for it when you take a train or a bus and when you go to a museum, a national monument, a theater, a movie, and anyplace else that charges admission.

There's also a Tourist Pass available for all ages, which offers free unlimited travel on Lisbon's transportation system. Sold at the airport and tourist information offices, a four-day pass costs about $10.

The Lisbon Card gives you the same access to the underground, buses, trains, and lifts, plus free entry into 25 museums, monuments, and other sites. It also provides discounts on sightseeing tours, river cruises, and theatrical events. Porto, Portugal's second-largest city, offers the Passe Porto with similar benefits.

For information: Portuguese National Tourist Office, 590 Fifth Ave., New York, NY 10036; 212-354-4403.

SCANDINAVIA

Scandinavia—which includes Denmark, Finland, Norway, and Sweden—has many good deals for mature travelers. Here are some that are valid in all four countries. (Those that are unique to the individual countries are described under their own headings throughout this chapter).

The Scanrail Senior Pass is designed for visitors over the age of 60 and must be purchased here before your departure. It offers a significant discount on the cost of rail travel, first or second class, anywhere within the four countries for 5 days (to be used within 15 days), 10 days (within a month), or 21 days (within a month). Bonuses of this pass (some of which may constitute usage of a travel day) include free or discounted passage on ferries and half price on some cruise lines.

For information: Rail Europe; 1-800-4-EURAIL (800-438-7245).

You and other travelers can also save money in the Scandinavian countries by using hotel passes. The Nordic Hotelpass, for example, gives you discounts of up to 50 percent off the regular room rates at over 90 first-class hotels that are part of Choice Hotels International. The card, valid all year around, costs about $12 and must be purchased in advance. The Scan+ Hotel Cheque program provides vouchers for discounted rates at about 180 other hotels throughout Scandinavia and is valid May through September. The Scandic Holiday Cheque is a similar program.

SAS (Scandinavian Airlines System) not only gives passengers over the age of 62 a 10 percent discount on fares between North America and Europe, but also discounts domestic fares in Denmark, Norway, and Sweden for travelers over 65. Also, Finnair gives you a terrific deal on flights within Finland—70 to 75 percent off the regular fares—if you are over 65. You must pay for your tickets within three days of booking.

And finally, you should seriously consider buying city cards for free public transportation plus free or discounted entry to museums, historic sites, and cultural attractions.

They can be purchased ahead of time in the U.S. or at tourist information offices, train stations, airports, and hotels in Scandinavia. The cities include Copenhagen, Odense, and Aalborg in Denmark; Helsinki in Finland; Oslo and Bergen in Norway; and Stockholm, Gothenburg, and Malmo in Sweden.

For information: Scandinavian National Tourist Offices, 655 Third Ave., New York, NY 10017; 212-885-9700.

SPAIN

In addition to discounts for mature travelers at just about every museum, cultural event, and historic site in Spain, there is another good deal for visitors over 60. The Golden Days Promotion offers a 35 percent discount on the cost of a room and buffet breakfast at the country's famous paradores. These are government-owned inns, 87 in all, many of them former palaces, castles, convents, or monasteries, located in the Spanish countryside. The discounted rates apply all year except in July, August, September, and Easter and Christmas weeks. Some paradores are available every day of the week; others only from Sunday to Thursday; and still others only on Friday, Saturday, and Sunday.

For information: Tourist Office of Spain, 666 Fifth Avenue, New York, NY 10103; 212-265-8822. For paradores: Marketing Ahead, 800-223-1356.

SWEDEN

If you plan to travel within Sweden, you may be wise to invest in the travel card sold by SJ, the state railroad system, which then gives you substantial discounts on train trips. Although the card is valid every day, the discounted seats are limited and you must book your trip at least seven days in advance. The card currently costs about $21, unless you are over 65. Then you'll pay only about $7 for the same privileges.

Hop on a bus in Sweden and, if you're 65, you need only pay half of the regular adult fare.

For seeing the sights in Stockholm, consider buying the SL Tourist Card sold at tourist offices and kiosks, again at half price for seniors (about $10 for three days). With this card, you get free transportation on buses, local trains, subways, and ferry tours.

Plan an overnight cruise from Stockholm to Finland on the Viking Line, or a one-day cruise from Gothenburg to Denmark on the Stena Line, and, if you are 60, the cost is much less than the regular adult fare.

SAS, the Scandinavian airline, takes 10 percent off the regular fares for passengers over 62 flying from this side of the Atlantic to SAS destinations worldwide. On flights within Sweden, the airline offers special senior fares, depending on the route, to passengers 65 and older.

And don't forget the city cards—the Stockholm Card, Gothenburg Card, and Malmo Card. Very good deals, they give you free or discounted transportation and admission to places you'll want to visit.

For information: Swedish Tourist Board, 655 Fifth Avenue, New York, NY 10017; 212-885-9700.

SWITZERLAND

The Swiss Hotel Association will provide, for the asking, a list of about 400 hotels in 160 cities and towns that participate in a program called *Season for Seniors*. This program reduces the room rates—sometimes as much as 50 percent—for women over 62 and men over 65. If two people are traveling together, only one must be the required age. The only catch is that in most cases the reduced rates do not apply during peak travel periods, including the summer months.

The Swiss Museum Passport is good for a month of unlimited visits to about 180 museums. If you are a woman over 62 or a man over 65, you may buy it at a discount at participating museums and tourist offices in Switzerland.
For information: Switzerland Tourism, 608 Fifth Ave., New York, NY 10022; 212-757-5944.

5

Trips and Tours for the Mature Traveler

Many enterprising organizations, tour operators, and travel agencies now cater exclusively to the mature traveler. They choose destinations sure to appeal to those who have already seen much of the world, arrange trips that are leisurely and unhassled, give you congenial contemporaries to travel with and group hosts to smooth the way, and provide many special services you never got before. They also give you a choice between strenuous action-filled tours and those that are more relaxed. In fact, most of the agencies offer so many choices that the major problem becomes making a decision about where to go.

Options range from cruises in the Caribbean or the Greek Isles to grand tours of the Orient, sight-seeing excursions in the United States, trips to the Canadian Rockies, theater tours of London, African safaris, and snorkeling vacations on the Great Barrier Reef off Australia. There's just no place in the world where over-50s won't go.

Among the newer and most popular trends are apartment/hotel complexes in American and European resort areas, as well as apartments in major cities. Here you can stay put for as long as you like, using the apartment or hotel as a home base for short-range roaming and exploring with the guidance of on-site hosts.

To qualify for some of the trips, one member of the party must meet the minimum age requirement, while the others may be younger.

TRIPS FOR THE MATURE TRAVELER

ADVENTURE HOLIDAYS

If you're looking for a bit of adventure and want to travel with a small companionable group of people who are at least 35 years old, consider the 13-day tours of New Zealand offered by Mid-Life Adventures. Scheduled for departures during New Zealand's summer—October through mid-April—you'll have moderately paced outdoor experiences as you travel all over the North or South Islands—or both—seeing the sights and visiting five national and two maritime parks. Owned by "a mature couple" and led by "mature" guides, this agency will take you sailing, white-water rafting, sea kayaking, cave rafting, sight-seeing, hiking, and on glacier walks, bush walks, and scenic flights, for which you need no previous experience but must be in good physical shape.

For information: Adventure Holidays, 2817 Wilshire Blvd., Santa Monica, CA 90403; 800-528-6129 or 310-998-5880.

AFC TOURS

Specializing in escorted tours designed for mature travelers, AFC schedules trips to all the most popular destinations in the U.S. and Canada and some in other countries. Not only that, but if you live in southern California, where AFC is based, you will be transported between your home and the airport. Domestic tours take you to such places as the national parks, Washington, D.C., Branson, Nashville, New York City, Savannah, and New Orleans. International adventures cover all of Europe. Other choices: cruises, steamboating, train tours, holiday tours, and grandparent trips. In other words, almost anything you want. Special for singles: If you sign up four months in advance and a roommate cannot be found to share your room, you need not pay a single supplement.

For information: AFC Tours, 11772 Sorrento Valley Rd., San Diego, CA 92121; 800-369-3693 or 619-481-8188.

BACK-ROADS TOURING CO.

Designed especially for adults over 50, the tours planned by Back-Roads Touring Co. take groups of no more than 11 participants on explorations of England, Scotland, Wales, Ireland, or France, along the back roads to out-of-the-way places. You'll travel by minicoach with a trained guide for one or two weeks, lodge in country inns, guest houses, and small family-owned properties. These are leisurely tours with plenty of time to explore. You'll stay several nights in the same location, and spend time with local residents. You may even help plan the itinerary. Add-on stays in London are available, too, and so are four-day "country breaks" and day trips out of London. What's more, if you mention this book, you will get a discount.

KEEP POSTED ON PERKS

Full of money-saving suggestions, useful advice, and tips on travel bargains, *The Thrifty Traveler* is a 12-page monthly news-letter with a special section that focuses on news for the over-50 traveler. It keeps track of the perks and celebrates the positives of getting older. Subscription: $29 a year.
For information: The Thrifty Traveler, PO Box 8168, Clearwater, FL 33758; 800-532-5731 or 727-447-4731; www.thriftytraveler.com.

A new specialty of this touring company is its Battles for France tour which starts in London, proceeds to General Eisenhower's headquarters in Portsmouth, crosses the channel, and visits famous battlefields in Normandy.
For information: Back-Roads Touring Co., British Network Ltd., 594 Valley Rd., Upper Montclair, NJ 07043; 800-274-8583 or 973-744-8814. In Canada, contact Golden Escapes, 75 The Donway West, Ste. 710, Toronto, ON M3C 2E9; 800-668-9125 or 416-447-7683.

CIE TOURS INTERNATIONAL

An agency whose trips go only to Ireland, Scotland, Wales, and England, CIE offers motorcoach tours and fly/drive vacations, some of which come with a 55 and Smiling Discount. This means that on certain departure dates you get $55 off the cost of the trip if you are 55 or older and are among the first 15 people to book the tour.
For information: CIE Tours International, 100 Hanover Ave., Cedar Knolls, NJ 07927; 800-243-8687 or 973-292-3438.

COLLETTE TOURS

The worry-free vacations for the mature population from Collette Tours, an escorted-tour operator for the last 80 years, include over 125 itineraries in seven continents. It even offers grand tours of South America or East Asia. Its trips move at a relaxed pace, put you up in good hotels, and provide experienced tour guides to see that everything goes well. In such places as Costa Rica, Denmark, Scotland, Portugal, Spain, Switzerland, Israel, and Austria, the agency's "Hub and Spoke" programs feature multiple nights in one place so you don't have to keep packing and un-packing your bags. Meanwhile, day excursions take you to see the sights.

The soft adventures from Collette are for people who love convenience but don't want to be overly organized as they tour the Galapagos, go on safari in Africa, take a trek through the Brazilian rain forest, or view the penguins in Antarctica.

For information: Collette Tours, 162 Middle St., Pawtucket, RI 02860; 800-832-4656.

CORLISS TOURS

The Stay-Put Tours by Corliss are planned with older travelers in mind—you fly to your destination, check into your hotel, hang up your clothes, and stay put, never pack-ing your bags again until it's time to go home. Meanwhile, you go on local tours and day trips to interesting places nearby. Each tour carries along a tour director who makes all the arrangements and shepherds the group around. Plenty of time, too, to relax and explore on your own.

Destinations include Atlanta, Orlando, Washington, D.C., New York, Philadelphia, San Antonio, Seattle, Denver, Colorado Springs, Nashville, New Orleans, Montreal, Plymouth, Chicago, Toronto, Ottawa, Calgary, and Vancouver. Each tour lasts a week, but you may link two or more trips as you like.

This agency also organizes holiday tours, many of them "Stay-Puts," over the Thanksgiving and Christmas holidays, taking you to resorts, festivals, and popular vacation destinations such as San Antonio, New Orleans, Branson, Myrtle Beach, and Scottsdale.

For information: Corliss Tours, 5950 Canoga Ave., Woodland Hills, CA 91367; 800-482-4597 or 818-999-0304.

DELTA QUEEN STEAMBOAT CO.

Steamboating, always popular among mature travelers, is the specialty of this company, whose steam-powered overnight paddle-wheelers ply the Mississippi River and other inland waterways on 3- to 14-night cruises. Among other offerings are big band cruises; a Dixie fest; voyages for Civil War buffs with lectures by historians and visits to battle sites; 1950s dance tours; Mark Twain cruises; a Kentucky Derby cruise; a Cajun culture cruise; and "Year That Was" trips celebrating 1946, 1948, or 1950.

For information: Delta Queen Steamship Co., Robin Street Wharf, 1380 Port of New Orleans Pl., New Orleans, LA 70130; 800-543-1949 or 504-586-0631.

ELDERTREKS

If you insist on viewing the world through bus windows and sleeping in five-star hotels, stop reading now, because on ElderTreks' adventures you'll be doing a lot of walking and you may sleep in a tribal village. ElderTreks is a program of all-inclusive adventure getaways open to anyone 50 and over (and companions of any age) who is in reasonably good physical condition and capable of walking at a steady pace in tropical conditions. Featuring exotic adventures to relatively remote places in the world, it stresses cultural interaction, physical activity, and nature exploration. However, itineraries are chosen with older hikers in mind and groups are limited to 15. Trekking portions of the trips are rated on physical difficulty and are optional. You may also choose a guesthouse-based itinerary.

Accommodations for the city portions of the tours are in clean, comfortable, tourist-class hotels and guesthouses chosen for charm and location. Accommodations on the adventure portions may be on the floor of a nomadic tent or under a canopy of trees in the jungle, but you can always count on having an air mattress to sleep on. Guides, cooks, meals, and porters are part of the package. Destinations include Thailand, Borneo, Vietnam, Laos, Sumatra, Java, Bali, China, Tibet, Nepal, India, Turkey, Ecuador and the Galapagos Islands, Costa Rica, Bolivia, Peru, Madagascar, Morocco, Yemen, Iceland, New Zealand, and Belize.

By the way, if you are traveling alone and are willing to share, you can avoid a single-supplement charge.

For information: ElderTreks, 597 Markham St., Toronto, ON M6G 2L7; 800-741-7956 or 416-588-5000.

FANCY-FREE HOLIDAYS

Geared for senior travelers, this agency's domestic escorted motorcoach tours include all of the usual favorite destina-

OVERSEAS RETIREMENT NETWORK

If you are looking for the perfect place to retire abroad but don't know where to start, consider taking a relocation tour to Central America with the Overseas Retirement Network to look at some possibilities. The tours, currently in Mexico, Costa Rica, Dominican Republic, Belize, and Honduras, vary from two to eight days and include seminars and workshops with expert speakers, introductions to Americans who have already made the move, and a close-up look at the country's special attractions. You will get a 10 percent discount from ORN if you mention you read about it here.

For information: Overseas Retirement Network, 2216 Troy Road, Edwardsville, IL 62025; 888-535-5289 or 618-659-0183.

tions such as Branson, New England, Alaska, Williamsburg, Asheville, New Orleans, and Washington, D.C. Its fully escorted overseas tours by air, motorcoach, or cruise ship include Ireland, Kenya, Spain, Greece, Germany, and South America. A special feature: most domestic motorcoach tours are fully refundable right up to the day of departure.

For information: Fancy-Free Holidays, 24W 500 Maple Ave., Naperville, IL 60540; 800-421-3330 or 630-778-7010.

GALAXY TOURS

Nostalgic journeys for GIs are the specialty of Galaxy Tours, which takes former members of the U.S. armed forces and their families back to the places where they once served. The most popular tour for World War II veterans, called the GI Favorite, begins in the training areas in England, visits the invasion beaches of Normandy, then takes the route taken by General George Patton's Third Army into Luxembourg, Belgium, and Germany.

Other World War II tours follow the invasion of southern France from Nice up through the Rhone Valley into Alsace Lorraine and Germany; and the Italian invasion from North Africa across Sicily and through Italy.

Veterans of Pacific battles may choose to revisit Australia, New Zealand, the Philippines, China, Burma, or India. If you served in the Korean or Vietnam Wars, you too can find a tour that takes you back. Join a group tour, organize your own group, or go as an individual traveler.
For information: Galaxy Tours, PO Box 234, Wayne, PA 19087; 800-523-7287 or 610-964-8010.

GO AHEAD VACATIONS

Go Ahead Vacations, a division of EF Education, a company that has specialized for over 30 years in intercultural exchange and educational travel, plans a wide array of holidays exclusively for the mature crowd. Its European Leisure Program, designed for independent people who prefer not to be part of a group tour, takes you to popular cities on the Continent. Here you stay in a hotel, breakfast included, and manage your own holiday with the help of an on-site coordinator. If instead you choose an all-inclusive program, you will stay for a week or more in a resort hotel in such places as the Canary Islands, Crete, or Spain's Costa del Sol, where meals and sight-seeing are included. The third option from Go Ahead includes a wide range of traditional motorcoach tours and cruises to just about anywhere you've ever wanted to go.

If you request a roommate, you'll get one or have your single supplement reduced by half.

For information: Go Ahead Vacations, EF Center Boston, 1 Education St., Cambridge MA 02141; 800-242-4686.

GOLDEN AGE FESTIVAL TRAVEL

Another agency that caters to the mature crowd, this one offers tours to everywhere from Wildwood (New Jersey), Myrtle Beach, Nashville, Maine, and New York to the national parks, Las Vegas, Europe, Greece, and Hawaii—plus plenty of cruises. All packages are escorted and include accommodations, meals, and just about everything else.

In addition, Golden Age Festival offers an innovation— drive-to tours for individual travelers, allowing them to take advantage of group discounts that make the trips remarkably inexpensive. On these, all on the East Coast, you drive yourself to your destination—for example, Wildwood, Ocean City, Myrtle Beach, Newport and Mystic Seaport, Hilton Head, Williamsburg—and join others traveling on their own for meals, entertainment, and tours.

For information: Golden Age Festival Travel, 5501 New Jersey Ave., Wildwood Crest, NJ 08260; 800-257-8920 or 609-522-6316.

GOLDEN AGE TRAVELLERS

This over-50 club's specialty is discounted cruises on major cruise lines everywhere in the world, but it offers land tours from well-known tour operators as well. When you join the club ($10 or $15 per couple a year), you receive a quarterly newsletter with listings of upcoming sailings. Other inducements are tour escorts and bonus points. Single travelers may choose to be enrolled in the Roommates Wanted list to help them find companions to share cabins and costs. For members in the San Francisco and Sacramento areas, there are one-day travel shows where you may meet fellow travelers and share a snack.

Especially intriguing to mature travelers are this agency's long-stay trips. On these, you stay put—for example, in Spain, Portugal, Guatemala, Australia, Costa Rica, or Argentina—at the same hotel for two or three weeks, and, if you wish, take short side trips. The packages include air, hotel, and sometimes meals.

For information: Golden Age Travellers, Pier 27, the Embarcadero, San Francisco, CA 94111; 800-258-8880 or 415-296-0151.

GOLDEN ESCAPES

Golden Escapes for the 50-Plus Traveller is a Canadian tour operator that offers all-inclusive escorted tours in Canada, the U.S., and Europe as well as three-week tours of such exotic places as Greece, Egypt, Cyprus, Turkey, Tunisia, and South Africa. It also has long-stay programs where you lodge in an apartment or a hotel in a resort area—perhaps Portugal's Algarve, Newport Beach, Palm Springs, or the island of Crete—and take excursions by day, highlighted by parties, happy hours, entertainment, and other activities.

In addition, Golden Escapes is the representative in Canada for Back-Roads Touring Co., which takes you on minicoach tours of England, France, Scotland, or Ireland. *For information:* Golden Escapes, 75 The Donway West, Ste. 710, Toronto, ON M3C 2E9; 800-668-9125 or 416-447-7683.

GRAND CIRCLE TRAVEL

Grand Circle caters to people over 50 and plans all of its trips exclusively for them. The first U.S. company to market senior travel, it specializes in extended vacations, escorted tours, and cruises. On an extended vacation, you get round-trip airfare from your gateway city to a foreign country. Then you stay in one, two, or three destinations for as many weeks as you like, living in hotels or apartments with all meals, sight-seeing tours, social events, and an on-site program director included. Meanwhile you may spend your days as you wish, joining the rest of the group or not.

Traditional escorted programs are also offered taking you to a variety of destinations with experienced guides. Everything is included from airfare to tours and many meals.

Traditional cruises are another choice, as are train tours and river cruises on small chartered boats on such rivers as the Danube, Rhine, Yangtze, and Nile.

Or look into the Discovery Series. These are educational travel trips designed to immerse you in the local culture, history, art, environment, and politics of a foreign country. You visit local families, take language lessons, learn to cook regional foods.

Grand Circle tries to match singles with appropriate roommates if they request them. If none are available, you will be charged only half the single supplement for your own room. On several of the extended-stay departure dates, there are no single supplements at all.

For information: Grand Circle Travel, 347 Congress St., Boston, MA 02210; 800-248-3737 or 617-350-7500. Ask for the free booklet *101 Tips for Mature Travelers.*

LIBERTY TRAVEL

The Mexico Seniors Program from Liberty Travel was created especially for travelers age 60 and over. The special packages take you on beach vacations to your choice of any of the most popular Mexican resort areas. Or, if you prefer city vacations, there are packages for Mexico City, Guadalajara, or Oaxaca. You must stay a minimum of two nights but may stay as long as you like. What makes these trips special for seniors are the bonuses, which vary from hotel to hotel but may include room upgrades, discounts on food and beverages, free night stays, or free breakfast.

For information: Liberty Travel, 800-764-1000.

MATURE TOURS

Mature Tours specializes in travel for "youthful spirits" over the age of 50 who wish to roam the world with other travelers in their own age group. A division of Solo Flights, which has a long history of catering to single voyagers of all ages, it welcomes both solo seniors and couples on its trips. Regular destinations include Costa Rica, Spain, and New York City. Also frequently on its schedule: steamboat cruises on the Mississippi River, some with add-on stays in New Orleans.

For information: Mature Tours, 10 Tait's Mill Rd., Trumbull, CT 06611; 800-266-1566 or 203-445-0107.

MAYFLOWER TOURS

Most of Mayflower's travelers are "55 or better," so the pace of its tours is leisurely and rest stops are scheduled every couple of hours. You travel by motorcoach, stay in good hotels or motels, and eat many of your meals together. All trips are fully escorted by tour directors who make sure all goes well. If you are a single traveler and request a roommate at least 30 days before departure, you'll get a roommate or a room to yourself with no single supplement to pay. Tours go almost everywhere in the United States and Canada, including national parks of the Southwest, the Canadian Rockies and Pacific Northwest, French Canada, Branson and the Ozarks, New England and Cape Cod, Hawaii, and New York. Cruises take you to the Caribbean, the Panama Canal, Alaska, Hawaii, or the New England coast.

For information: Mayflower Tours, 1225 Warren Ave., Downers Grove, IL 60515; 800-323-7604 or 630-960-3430.

PETRABAX VACATIONS

An agency that specializes in escorted tours for mature travelers, Petrabax offers a 50 percent price reduction for travel companions from December through March on the land portion of many of its six-night programs in Spain and Portugal. Additional weeks in first-class hotels are available at low cost in resorts on the Costa del Sol or the Algarve, both known for mild winter climates. A Spanish tour begins in Madrid and then travels by motorcoach to Córdoba, Seville, and the Costa Del Sol. A Portugal program provides three nights in Lisbon and three in the Algarve.

For information: Petrabax Vacations, 97–45 Queens Blvd., Rego Park, NY 11374; 800-634-1188.

PLEASANT HAWAIIAN HOLIDAYS

To people at least 55 years old, many of Pleasant's hotels and condos all over the Hawaiian islands offer either a free room upgrade or an upgrade with free breakfast; plus car-rental upgrades and discount certificates for activities and events. Called the *Makua Club*, the program is free and only one person per room needs to be 55.

For information: Pleasant Hawaiian Holidays, 2404 Townsgate Rd., Westlake, CA 91361; 800-2-HAWAII (800-242-9244) or 818-991-3390.

RFD TOURS

Created many years ago to arrange visits between American and foreign farmers, and then to organize flower and garden tours, RFD Travel now plans a wide range of U.S. and international tours and cruises every year specifically for mature travelers. All hosted, the trips stress cultural heritage events, personal encounters with local residents, knowledgeable tour managers, and an easy pace.

For information: RFD Tours, 1225 Warren Ave., Downers Grove, IL 60515; 800-365-5359 or 630-960-3974.

SAGA HOLIDAYS

Saga plans trips exclusively for travelers over 50. It offers an astonishing variety of vacations, from fully escorted, all-inclusive tours of any place you've ever wanted to visit to cruises and safaris, educational travel, walking tours, and winter resort stays. It also offers grand tours of Europe, holidays in Turkey or Greece, nature tours of Borneo, and river cruises down the Danube River or the Yangtze River in China.

All-inclusive resort holidays are designed to let you live a while in one place—in Portugal, Spain, Sicily, Costa Rica, Ecuador, Nicaragua, Turkey, or Greece—where you settle into your hotel for a relaxing stay-put vacation that includes entertainment, activities, and excursions.

In 1996, Saga introduced the *Saga Rose*, its own ship, and a variety of voyages in European waters. The only ship that caters exclusively to over-50s, its itineraries and amenities are tailored for mature customers.

Associated with Saga, too, are two educational travel programs. Smithsonian Odyssey Tours, in partnership with the famed Smithsonian Institution, gives you a wide choice of learning adventures guided by experts in their fields. Among recent choices: Egypt's ancient temples, the Mayan culture, the mysteries of Machu Picchu, Moorish castles in Spain and Portugal, imperial Russian waterways, and the cultural treasures of Ireland.

The Road Scholar program offers travel-study itineraries each with a special theme, such as French impressionism, British mystery novels, the geology of Iceland, the paintings and palaces of St. Petersburg, and Dutch and Flemish art. Each trip includes lectures by experts from academic or cultural institutions, plus excursions and activities.

Saga schedules singles-only departures and tours with no single supplements on many of its itineraries so that solo participants pay the same amount per person as twosomes. In addition, there is no extra charge or merely a modest one for singles on many of its other tours. The company will also try to match travelers with roommates, if requested, for savings and companionship. For land vacations, a roommate is guaranteed or there is no extra charge if one is not available.

For information: Saga Holidays, 222 Berkeley St., Boston, MA 02116; 800-343-0273. Smithsonian Odysseys: 800-258-5885. Road Scholar programs: 800-621-2151. *Saga Rose*: 800-952-9590.

SCI/NATIONAL RETIREES OF AMERICA

This agency, which began decades ago with trips to the Catskills resorts, now offers a long list of escorted group tours for seniors that range from 1-day outings to 45-day world cruises. The land tours—5-day jaunts by air to Las Vegas are its specialty—depart midweek, transport you by motorcoach, and take you to such places as New Orleans, Quebec, Niagara Falls, the Poconos, Orlando, Nashville, or New York.

For information: SCI/National Retirees of America, 1188

MEXICAN PREVIEW

A California travel company, **Barvi Tours**, conducts a weekly five-night trip to Guadalajara, a popular retirement city in Mexico, for those who are contemplating retirement there. Here you tour the residential areas of Chapala and Ajijic on the shore of the largest lake in Mexico, explore the area, talk to residents, and learn from experts about cultural differences, personal finances, medical services, housing, immigration laws, cost of living, and shopping.

For information: Barvi Tours, 11658 Gateway Blvd., Los Angeles, CA 90064; 800-824-7102 or 310-474-4041.

Grand Ave., Baldwin, NY 11510; 800-698-1101 or 516-485-3200.

SENIORITY ADVENTURES

These trips, all originating from Houston, Texas, take groups of seniors on motorcoach tours and cruises to some of their favorite destinations in the U.S., such as Branson, Washington, D.C., New England, the Caribbean, and Alaska. One of Seniority's specialties is short trips close to home in the vast state of Texas: Big Bend country, Aransas National Wildlife Refuge to spot whooping cranes, and Tyler to see the roses. It also offers a few adventures to foreign lands.

For information: Seniority Adventures, PO Box 709, Sugar Land, TX 77487; 800-256-0105 or 281-491-6565.

SOPHISTICATED VOYAGES

A sister company to Grandtravel, Sophisticated Voyages operates one or two upscale tours a year for older travelers who want a relaxed itinerary rich in cultural activities, outstanding meals, fine hotels, and plenty of free time. What they don't want are hassles, large groups, all-day bus rides, hurried breakfasts, and many events crammed into the day. Current trips include a 10-day Britain tour that combines 5 nights in London with 3 nights at Thornbury Castle in County Avon; and a two-week safari in Kenya where you are lodged in elegant hotels, lodges, and tented camps.

For information: Sophisticated Voyages, 6900 Wisconsin Ave., Chevy Chase, MD 20815; 800-247-7651 or 301-986-0790.

TRAFALGAR TOURS

After 50 years of taking Americans on tours of Europe, Trafalgar has now added a first-class tour program in the U.S. and Canada with more than a dozen regional itineraries. Catering to older travelers who want to see the sights without worrying about logistics and details, these escorted motorcoach tours include luxury coaches, first-class hotels or lodges, guided sight-seeing, gratuities, and most meals. Trafalgar also continues its overseas tours, both first-class and budget, to Europe, Britain, and South Africa. Traveling alone? You'll be matched with an appropriate roommate. *For information:* Trafalgar Tours USA, 11 East 16 St., New York, NY 10010-1402; 800-854-0103 or 212-725-7776.

VALUE WORLD TOURS

An agency that specializes in trips to central and eastern Europe, Value World Tours takes 10 to 20 percent off the cost of some of its tours and river cruises on some off-peak departure dates for travelers over the age of 50. River cruises include trips on inland waterways in Russia, Ukraine, central Europe, and China, while the hosted or escorted motorcoach tours go to many destinations in the same parts of the world. The two-week programs may be extended before or after the trips. *For information:* Value World Tours, 17220 Newhope St., Fountain Valley, CA 92708; 800-795-1633 or 714-556-8258.

VANTAGE DELUXE WORLD TRAVEL

Vantage features upscale tours for mature travelers and since 1983 has escorted more than a quarter of a million over-

50 tourists around the world on land tours and cruises. Accommodations are always deluxe and explorations are leisurely and relaxed, so there is plenty of time to savor the sights. All trips are led by tour directors who see to it that everything—from ticketing and baggage handling to check-ins, meals, and tips—is taken care of for you. Among Vantage's most popular tours are a Danube River cruise, a trip through the Panama Canal, a visit to China and the Yangtze River, and an exploration of Ireland or the countries of Eastern Europe. There are also longer, more exotic trips such as a deluxe around-the-world tour.

If you are traveling alone and want a roommate, a compatible companion will be found or half the single supplement on land programs will be waived.

For information: Vantage Deluxe World Travel, 111 Cypress St., Brookline, MA 02445; 800-784-0935. Ask for the free booklets *99 Travel Tips for Mature Travellers* and *Health Guide for Older Travellers.*

VISTA TOURS

Another agency providing escorted tours almost exclusively for the mature set, Vista Tours plans leisurely trips with plenty of stops and ample time to enjoy the points of interest and relax too. You travel on comfortable motorcoaches with escorts who deal with the reservations, transfers, luggage, meal arrangements, and all other potentially problematic situations. Destinations, although mainly in the U.S., also include Canada, Europe, and Hawaii. A highlight every year is a five-day trip over the New Year's holiday to California for the Pasadena Rose Parade and a New Year's Eve party with a big band and a celebrity show. If you're a woman who doesn't have a dancing partner or wants a better one, you may take your turn whirling around the floor with one of the gentleman hosts who accompany the group.

For information: Vista Tours, 1923 N. Carson St., Ste. 105, Carson City, NV 89701; 800-647-0800.

CRUISING THE OCEANS, RIVERS, AND SEAS

Cruises have always appealed to the mature crowd. In fact, the majority of passengers on most sailings are over the age of 50, if not 60. So you are sure to find suitable companionship. However, never sign up for a vacation at sea without shopping around for a discount because you rarely have to pay the advertised rate. Work with your own travel agent or call a discount cruise agency such as The Cruise Line (800-777-0707) or World Wide Cruises (800-882-9000) to search out the best deals available when and where you want to travel.

In the meantime, for starters, here are some senior specials designed especially for you.

BALLROOM DANCERS WITHOUT PARTNERS

Are you a single man or woman who loves to dance? Look into the many cruises scheduled every year by this agency that caters to solo travelers over 50—no couples allowed. Both beginner and accomplished dancers learn new steps during the day before dinner, and, elegantly dressed, dance again until midnight after dinner and a show. One male host, an excellent dancer, goes along for every five passengers in the group. BDWP will arrange cabin shares so you can avoid the single surcharge. Both big bands and Latin rhythms are featured, and itineraries take you everywhere from the Caribbean to Mexico and Alaska.

For information: Ballroom Dancers Without Partners, 651 NW 31 St., Miami, FL 33127; 800-778-7953 or 305-637-4777.

BERGEN LINE

The cruises in Scandinavia of Color Line and Norwegian Coastal Voyages, both represented in the U.S. by Bergen Line, offer special discounts to older travelers.

Color Line, Norway's largest cruise passenger company that cruises the North Sea and travels to England and the Continent, gives travelers over 60 and a companion half-price on standard fares on many of its sailings.

Norwegian Coastal Voyages, with ships that take you along Norway's spectacular coast from Bergen to Kirkenes, above the Arctic Circle, and back, gives a break to passengers over the age of 67. It takes about $200 per person off the 12-day 2,500-mile round-trip fare, and about $100 per person off the 6- or 7-day one-way fare all year except between June 1 and July 15.

For information: Bergen Line, 800-323-7436 or 212-319-1300.

B&V WATERWAYS

Choose a cruise on a deluxe hotel barge on the canals and waters of Europe and you will get a discount of 10 percent if you are a member of AARP. Take your pick of fully crewed and all-inclusive barge trips in Ireland, France, Holland, or England.

For information: B&V Waterways, 800-999-3636.

CARNIVAL CRUISE LINES

You're entitled to savings on many of Carnival's cruises if you belong to AARP. You can save $200 per stateroom in categories 6 through 12 on long cruises to Alaska and other

MERRY WIDOWS DANCE CRUISES

Designed for solo women from 50 to 90 who love to dance but don't have partners, **Merry Widows Dance Tours** runs many cruises every year to such places as the Caribbean, Southeast Asia, Alaska, Greece and the Mediterranean, and the Panama Canal. The trips range from 7 days to 18. Sponsored by the AAA Auto Club South, the cruises take along their own gentleman hosts, one professional dancer for every four women. Each woman receives a dance card that rotates her partners every night throughout the cruise, whether she's a beginner or a polished dancer. The men are also rotated at the dinner tables so everyone gets the pleasure of their company. You don't have to be a widow and you don't even have to know the cha-cha or the macarena to enjoy these trips. If you are traveling alone and wish to avoid paying a single supplement, you will be assigned a roommate.

Merry Widows also operates tours to major resorts, in such settings as the Cloister in Georgia's Sea Islands and the Lawrence Welk Resort in Branson. Out-of-the-country resort destinations include European capitals, the Greek Isles and Turkey, Tahiti, Hawaii, and the Caribbean.

For information: Call your travel agent or contact Merry Widows Dance Tours, 1515 N. Westshore Blvd., Tampa, FL 33607; 800-313-7245.

destinations; $100 per stateroom on 7-day voyages to the Caribbean or the Mexican Riviera; $50 on shorter trips to the Bahamas or Baja, Mexico. Your membership number must be provided when your trip is booked.

For information: Carnival Cruise Lines, 800-CARNIVAL (800-227-6482).

EUROCRUISES

If you are 55 or older, you—and a companion traveling with you—qualify for a 25 percent reduction on the published fares on several sailings of the four-star, 797-passenger *Black Watch* operated by Fred. Olsen Cruise Lines. The SeniorSavers departures—with Norwegian officers and an English cruise staff—currently sail from Dover, England, and take you to Norway, the Baltic Sea, or Barbados. Included are special escorts, cocktail parties, get-togethers for singles, a party, and a gentleman-host program that provides dancing partners for women traveling alone.

For information: EuroCruises, 303 W. 13th St., New York, NY 10014; 800-688-3876 or 212-691-2099.

HOLLAND AMERICA LINE

If you are a member of AARP and book an outside cabin on a Holland America cruise or Alaska cruise tour of seven days or longer, you can save $100 per stateroom. On shorter cruises, the savings is $50 per stateroom. Single travelers save half those amounts. To get the discounts, your membership number must be provided when your trip is booked.

For information: Holland America Line, 800-887-3529.

KD RIVER CRUISES OF EUROPE

Here you're in luck if you are celebrating a big anniversary. This company, the oldest and biggest river cruise line in Europe, takes 25 percent off the bill for couples celebrating their 25th, 40th, 50th, or 60th anniversaries on most of its sailings on the Rhine, the Danube, or the Elbe Rivers in central Europe. The anniversary needn't coincide with the cruise departure date—it just has to take place some time in the same year. A marriage certificate or other proof of the wedding date is required.

For information: KD River Cruises of Europe, 800-346-6525 or 914-696-3600 in the eastern U.S.; 800-858-8587 or 415-392-8817 in the western U.S., including Alaska and Hawaii.

RENAISSANCE CRUISES

If you are at least 50 and a member of AARP, you can save $100 per member on all cabin categories on Renaissance "R-Series" cruises in the Mediterranean, Greek Isles, and South Pacific. This is the first cruise line to feature direct booking by telephone or on-line.

For information: Renaissance Cruises, 800-525-5350.

ROYAL CARIBBEAN INTERNATIONAL

Check with your travel agent to find out when this cruise line will be offering one of its special promotions for seniors, because the cost on these sailings, many of them scheduled in the off-peak seasons, is always less than the lowest standard discounted rates. If one passenger in your cabin is over the age of 55, your cabin mates each get the same deal. Because cruises have special appeal to the older pop-

ulation, RCI's brochures indicate the activity level and amount of walking on each shore excursion.
For information: Royal Caribbean International, 800-327-6700.

ROYAL HAWAIIAN CRUISES

These day trips—some of them luncheon or dinner cruises—take you out on small ships (*Navatek I* or *Navatek II*), famous for their comfort and smooth ride; or adventure rafts (*Maui Nui Explorer* or *Na Pali Explorer*), more rugged and designed for ecotourism. You'll sail along exclusive routes for exploring, snorkeling, whale watching, and sight-seeing in the Hawaiian Islands. If you are over 65, you'll get a 15 percent discount on all day trips. Mention your age when you make your reservations.
For information: Royal Hawaiian Cruises, 800-852-4183.

SAGA ROSE

The voyages of the *Saga Rose*, the 580-passenger cruise ship now owned by Saga Holidays, caters exclusively to travelers over the age of 50. Based in England, the ship cruises to Iceland, Scandinavia, the Arctic Circle, Spain, the Canary Islands, and the Baltic cities. It also makes a 99-night trip around the world.
For information: Saga Holidays, 800-952-9590.

SENIORS AT SEA

Through Seniors at Sea you get a special group rate when you book a cruise with up to 30 people over the age of 50. You will sail aboard a first-class cruise line to such popular destinations as Alaska, the Panama Canal, the Mediterranean, or northern Europe and Russia. Your group dines together every evening and is accompanied by two knowledgeable guides who conduct shipboard seminars on the history, culture, art, geology, and wildlife of the areas you will visit. This way you'll know what you're looking at when you get there.

For information: Seniors at Sea, 107 222 St. SW, Bothell, WA 98021; 800-453-9283.

WORLD EXPLORER CRUISES

When the *S.S. Universe Explorer* is not serving as a floating university campus (see Chapter 16), it cruises to Alaska, the Caribbean, and Central and South America with on-board presentations on the history, wildlife, and culture of each of the ports visited. Members of AARP get a 20 percent discount on the brochure rates on all Alaska cruises (9 or 14 nights) in cabin categories 2 through 6. Single travelers pay a special supplement of 125 percent in the same categories, while friends and family cruise free in third and fourth berths, categories 3 through 5.

By the way, this ship features a computer lab with instructors from SeniorNet (see Chapter 16) who teach passengers everything from basic word processing to the Internet. The classes are free to SeniorNet members who pay the annual membership fee.

For information: World Explorer Cruises, 800-854-3835.

GENTLEMEN HOSTS

Because single men of a certain age are scarce among the traveling population, especially on board ship, a growing number of cruise lines offer almost free travel to carefully chosen unattached men over 45—in some cases, over 65—with excellent social and dancing skills. These gentlemen hosts serve as dancing or dining partners, make a fourth for bridge, act as escorts for shore trips, and socialize—without favoritism—with the single women on board.

There are stringent screening procedures and many more applicants than positions, so don't be surprised if you are not encouraged to apply. Hosts must provide their own wardrobes and sometimes their own airfare as well as a fee to the placement agency for every week at sea.

American Hawaii Cruises takes two dancing hosts on its Big Band cruises. On this cruise line that provides weekly seven-day cruises to four islands in Hawaii, the hosts, who are knowledgeable about the islands, mingle with the guests and help the single passengers enjoy their voyages and shore excursions.

For information: American Hawaii Cruises, Entertainment Dept., 2100 N. Nimitz Hwy., Honolulu, HI 96819.

Commodore Cruise Line's ship, *Enchanted Isle*, which sails every Saturday from the Port of New Orleans to Caribbean and Mexican ports, takes two or more male dance hosts on every cruise from August through April. Single, over-50, retired or semi-retired businessmen, their job is to attend all dance lessons and to dance with passengers to the music of an eight-piece orchestra each night of the seven-night voyage.

For information: Karp Enterprises, 1999 University Drive, Coral Springs, FL 33071; 954-341-9400.

Crystal Cruises, whose worldwide cruises carry three or four hosts per trip, look for personable social hosts over the age of 65 who are great dancers and enjoy keeping older single women passengers entertained both on board and ashore.

For information: Entertainment Dept., Crystal Cruises, 2121 Avenue of the Stars, Los Angeles, CA 90067.

Cunard Line's cruises aboard *Queen Elizabeth 2*, the *Vistafjord*, and the *Royal Viking Sun* carry along four to ten friendly gentleman hosts between the ages of 45 and 70. Their job is not only to whirl around the dance floor with women who need partners but to act as friendly diplomats who help passengers get to know one another. A knowledge of foreign languages is a plus.

For information: Working Vacation, 610 Pine Grove Ct., New Lenox, IL 60451; 815-485-8307.

The Delta Queen Steamboat Co., which makes about 50 cruises a year up and down the Mississippi River, taking you back in time aboard huge paddle wheelers, employs mature and responsible male hosts, assigning two to each trip on the *Mississippi Queen* and four to each Big Band cruise. Their job is to dance with the single women aboard, organize activities, and help everyone enjoy the voyage.

For information: Working Vacation, 610 Pine Grove Ct., New Lenox, IL 60451; 815-485-8307.

Holland America Line recruits retired professionals with good social skills to act as hosts on its long cruises and Big Band Sailings. Usually four to six hosts go along on each trip.

For information: Working Vacation, 610 Pine Grove Ct., New Lenox, IL 60451; 815-485-8307.

Merry Widows Dance Cruises offers many cruises and land tours for single, widowed, or divorced women who were born to dance. Accompanying them are gentleman hosts (one for every four women) to serve as dance partners.

For information: Merry Widows Dance Tours, 1515 N. West-shore Blvd., Tampa, FL 33607; 813-289-1444.

Orient Lines, whose ship, the 800-passenger *Marco Polo,* operates in the Far East, South Pacific, Indian Ocean, Mediterranean, and Antarctica, takes three or four gentlemen hosts along on all voyages except those in the Mediterranean. The hosts act as dance and dinner partners for the women passengers who are traveling on their own. Orient Lines also offers a guaranteed share program that matches singles with roommates so they may avoid the single supplement.
For information: Working Vacation, 610 Pine Grove Ct., New Lenox, IL 60451; 815-485-8307.

Premier Cruises assigns two hosts to every one of its many ships that cruise the Caribbean and the Canary Islands. The *Rembrandt* (formerly the *Rotterdam*) also carries these sociable gentlemen on its worldwide adventures, as does the *Big Red Boat* (except in the summer or during winter holiday weeks).
For information: Working Vacation, 610 Pine Grove Ct., New Lenox, IL 60451; 815-485-8307.

Royal Olympic Cruises takes two professional hosts on all of its cruises of seven days or longer. Their assignment is to dance with the women who love to dance but haven't brought partners with them.
For information: Cruise Crafts International; 407-365-4426.

Silversea Cruises has introduced gentlemen hosts aboard some of the sailings of the sister ships *Silver Cloud* and *Silver Wind.* The hosts' job is to dance, mingle, and mix, making sure all guests have an enjoyable voyage.

For information: Working Vacation, 610 Pine Grove Ct., New Lenox, IL 60451; 815-485-8307.

World Explorer Cruises: The *Universe Explorer*, whose summer ports are in Alaska and winter ports in the Caribbean and Central and South America, takes a couple of hosts along on all sailings.

For information: Working Vacation, 610 Pine Grove Ct., New Lenox, IL 60451; 815-485-8307.

6

Singles on the Road

More and more people of all ages book trips today unaccompanied and, to encourage and accommodate them, there are increasing numbers of tours planned exclusively for single travelers. Several major tour companies catering to mature travelers now schedule singles-only departures on which you mingle with others on their own, and many have reduced or even dropped the single-supplement charge on at least some of their tours so you may not have to pay for the privilege of a single room.

If, however, you are single, single again, or have a spouse who isn't the traveling kind and don't want to go places by yourself even in a group, consider joining a club that will help match you up with a fellow traveler who is also looking for a compatible person with whom to share adventures, a room, and expenses. Traveling with another person is usually more enjoyable and certainly less expensive than going alone because you share double accommodations, thereby avoiding the usual single supplement, which can be substantial.

TRAVEL COMPANION EXCHANGE

TCE specializes in helping single travelers find compatible travel partners. Managed by travel expert Jens Jurgen, Travel Companion Exchange is the largest, most enduring, and most successful matchmaking service. In fact, it has recently absorbed several other travel-partner services, including Golden Companions.

Members of TCE receive bulky bimonthly newsletters packed with travel tips and helpful advice plus long listings of people (TCE now has close to 3,000 active members) who are seeking new friends and/or travel partners of the same or opposite sex. For more information about those who seem to be good possibilities, you can send for full profiles (meanwhile, others send for yours) so you may judge their suitability for yourself. You do your own matchmaking. Jurgen suggests you talk by telephone, correspond, meet, and, even better, take a short trip together before setting out on a major adventure.

You may join TCE at an introductory fee of $99 for eight months or $159 for a year, using a credit card if you wish. By the way, you don't have to join TCE to subscribe to the *TCE Newsletter* (without the listings) for $48 per year. It is a gold mine of detailed travel news, tips, and bargains for all inveterate travelers, single or not.

For information: Travel Companion Exchange Inc., PO Box 833, Amityville, NY 11701; 800-392-1256 or 516-454-0880. Send $6 for a sample newsletter.

CONNECTING

A club based in Canada, Connecting is a "solo travel network" that aims to keep its 1,500-or-so single members—almost half of them over 50—in touch with each other, advising them on where to go, what to do, and how to enjoy their travel alone or with friends. Members, who pay an annual fee of $35 (Canadian) or $25 (U.S.), receive a lengthy newsletter six times a year. This newsletter, which devotes a whole section to mature travelers, includes unlimited free listings for members looking for compatible travel companions, reader recommendations and comments, and a directory of travel companies that offer special accommodations or programs for singles. An added benefit: you may participate in the Hospitality Program, which recruits volunteers to spend time—talking, sight-seeing, hiking, sharing a meal, whatever—with visiting members from other places. Other volunteers share their personal travel tips and tales.

For information: Connecting, PO Box 29088, 1996 W. Broadway, Vancouver, BC V6J 5C2, Canada; 800-557-1757 or 604-737-7791.

TOURS FOR SOLO TRAVELERS

Most tour operators and agencies specializing in escorted trips for people in their prime will try to find you a roommate (of the same sex) to share your room or cabin so you will not have to pay a single supplement. And, if they can't manage to find a suitable roommate for you, they will usually reduce the supplement or even cancel it. Some run singles-only trips too. In any case, keep in mind that you'll hardly have time or opportunity to be lonely on the typical escorted tour run by these agencies. If you are planning an extended stay in just one location, however, you may have more need for company.

For more about the tour operators listed below, see Chapter 5. Other companies may offer the same roommate-matching service, though they don't make a point of it, so always ask about it if you're interested.

GOING SOLO TRAVEL CLUB

A singles-only social club, Going Solo caters to unattached travelers of all ages but mainly to those on the far side of 50. Located in Calgary, Alberta, in Canada, it has many U.S. members and welcomes them all on its worldwide tours to places like the British Isles, Africa, Belize, Guatemala, Mexico, Turkey, and Greece.

The club also offers day trips, local social activities, and weekend getaways. Members, who pay an annual fee of $66.34 (Canadian), travel at group rates and are charged no single supplement fees.

For more information: Going Solo Travel Club, 187 Midlawn Close SE, Calgary, AB T2X 1A7; 888-446-7656 (outside Alberta) or 403-256-7871.

SOLO FLIGHTS

This agency makes it its business to know about the best tours, cruises, packages, groups, and rates for single people of all ages, and will suggest where to go on short holidays or lengthy vacations in the U.S. or abroad. It represents major tour operators and cruise lines and also offers its own package trips, some marketed by its affiliate, Mature Tours, exclusively for older travelers. One call or letter and you can find out what's out there that might possibly interest you. In return for the consultation, the agency hopes to do your booking.

For information: Solo Flights, 10 Tait's Mill Rd., Trumbull, CT 06611; 800-266-1566 or 203-445-0107.

SOLO'S HOLIDAYS

The UK's largest singles tour operator, Solo's Holidays offers hosted group vacations for unattached people. Although it is based in England, it will happily take Americans and Canadians on tour, giving them a chance to talk, dine, dance, and share experiences with other single travelers. All trips are divided into two groups, the first exclusively for ages 28 to 55, and the second for ages 45 to 69, although sometimes the ages are mixed.

For information: Solo's Holidays, 54-58 High St., Edgware, Middlesex HA8 7EJ, England; 0181-951-2828. E-mail: travel@solosholidays,co.uk.

TGIF VANCOUVER

A travel club for singles over 35, TGIF is based in Vancouver, B.C., but welcomes solo travelers from everywhere on its many getaway weekends and longer tours to other parts of the world. It maintains two calendars of events, one for members under 40, another for those over 40. Almost all of the club activities take place in or around Vancouver and include everything from dances to hikes, picnics, parties, weekend excursions, sailing trips, and theater nights. Recent organized travel tours—open to singles from elsewhere—have been to Mexico, Alaska, and the West Coast of California.

For information: TGIF Vancouver, 977 Wellington Dr., North Vancouver, B.C. V7K 1L1; 800-661-7151 or 604-980-2901.

HOOK-UPS FOR SOLO RVers

RVers who travel alone in their motor homes or vans can hook up with others in the same circumstances when they join one of the groups mentioned below. All of the clubs provide opportunities to travel together or to meet at campgrounds on the road, making friends with fellow travelers and having a fine time.

LONERS OF AMERICA

LOA is a club for single campers who want to travel together. Established in 1987, it currently has 29 chapters throughout the country and well over 800 active members from their 40s to their 90s, almost all retired and widowed, divorced, or otherwise single. Many of them live year-round in their motor homes or vans, and others hit the road only occasionally. They camp together, rally together, caravan together, often meeting at special campgrounds that cater to solo campers.

A not-for-profit member-operated organization, the club publishes a biannual membership directory and a lively monthly newsletter that keeps members in touch and informs them about campouts and rallies all over the country. The chapters organize their own events as well. Cur-

FOREVER YOUNG AT CLUB MED

For guests over the age of 55, Club Med takes $100 off the bill (except during major holidays) for stays of seven nights or more at any of its villages in the U.S., Mexico, the Caribbean, and French Polynesia. Choose from three varieties of resorts: Adult Villages (mainly for young singles), Family Villages (designed for families with children), or Villages for Everyone (the best bet for senior couples or singles). Inquire about hills, stairs, bathrooms, shopping, sports facilities, if these are some of your concerns, so you can decide on the best place for you.

For information: Club Med, 800-258-2633.

rently, dues are $40 a year plus a $5 registration fee for new members.

For information: Loners of America, PO Box 3314, Napa, CA 94558; 888-805-4562.

LONERS ON WHEELS

A camping and travel club for mature single campers, Loners on Wheels is not a lonely hearts club or a matchmaking service, but simply an association of friends and extended family. With 68 chapters located throughout the United States and Canada, LOW now has a membership of about 2,800 unpartnered travelers. The club schedules hundreds of camping events during the year at campgrounds, some of which are remote and cost little.

The club's newly acquired RV Ranch in Deming, N.M., (which also serves as its headquarters) offers special rates for club members, two rallies a year, dances and games in the clubhouse, and occasional forays into Mexico. A monthly newsletter and an annual directory keep everyone up to date and in touch.

Annual dues at this writing are $45 U.S. and $54 Canadian, plus a one-time enrollment fee of $5.

For information: Loners on Wheels, PO Box 1355, Poplar Bluff, MO 63902. Ask for a free sample newsletter.

FRIENDLY ROAMERS

Founded by former members of Loners on Wheels, Friendly Roamers is open to everyone, couples as well as singles, so friendships and RV activities can be continued despite a change of marital status or travel arrangements. Membership gets you admission to all club events, such as rallies and campouts, a newsletter, and a membership directory. Annual dues are $10 plus a one-time registration fee of $5 for new members. Local chapters hold their own events and join the others as well.

For information: Friendly Roamers, PO Box 2010, Sparks, NV 89432.

S*M*A*R*T

An RV club for retired members of the U.S. and Canadian armed forces, Special Military Active Retired Travel Club (S*M*A*R*T) sponsors caravans and gatherings for its 3,700 members in 45 chapters around the country and helps military bases improve their family campgrounds. Caravans have recently traveled to many destinations in the U.S., including Arkansas, Tennessee, and several Western states.

The club also tours such places as Australia, New Zealand, Tahiti, Great Britain, and Scandinavia, flying overseas and then touring on land in fully equipped rented RVs. To join, U.S. residents pay an initiation fee of $10 and then $25 a year per family; Canadian residents pay $15 (U.S.) and $30 (U.S.) per family, while associate members (disabled, former POWs, Medal of Honor recipients, widows or widowers of eligible members) pay a $10 initiation fee, then $12.50 a year.

For information: S*M*A*R*T Inc., 600 University Office Blvd., Pensacola, FL 32504; 800-354-7681.

RVing WOMEN

Women travelers who take to the highways in recreational vehicles can get advice and support from RVing Women, a club with over 4,000 female members. The group sponsors rallies, caravans, and other events across the U.S., Canada, and Mexico, plus weekend RV maintenance and RV driving classes in many locations around the country. Members pay an annual membership fee of $42 and receive a bimonthly magazine that covers topics such as safety, scams on the road, vehicle maintenance, and announcements of upcoming events and includes an annual directory of members.

For information: RVing Women, PO Box 1940, Apache Junction, AZ 85217; 888-55-RVING (888-557-8464) or 602-983-4678.

7

Airfares: Improving with Age

One thing that improves with your age is airfare. Almost every airline, domestic or foreign, gives people at either 60 or 62 and a traveling companion a 10 percent discount off any published fare. That may not be much of a deal, but it's certainly better than nothing.

Virtually every major U.S. airline also offers travelers over 62 booklets of four or eight coupons, each good for a one-way trip within the lower 48 states and sometimes beyond. The coupons are a good deal, though not as good as they used to be since airfare costs have been steadily increasing. However, on long flights they can save you considerable money when there are no fare sales going on.

They have other advantages too. For example, unlike other low-fare tickets that require round-trip reservations, those you get with your coupons let you fly one way and decide later when you want to return. That means there is no minimum-stay requirement. You don't have to stay over a Saturday night, and you must make your reservations only 14 days before departure. Another important point: you can use them for instant travel on a standby basis; this is infinitely cheaper than the usual last-minute fares.

Good as they are, senior coupons aren't always the best way to go. Four major U.S. carriers now have senior clubs, each with different offers and all of them definitely worth considering if you do a lot of flying. The cost of a flight, long or short, can be much less than a coupon price. Moreover, these clubs also offer cut-rate international travel that isn't available with the coupons. For details, check out United, American, Delta, and Continental in this chapter.

You get this variety of enticements because you, the mature population, have proved to be the hottest travel market around, a vast and growing group of careful consumers with money in your pockets and time on your hands midweek and in off-peak travel periods, just when the airlines are eager to fill up seats.

But, first, keep in mind:

■ Find a good travel agent and ask for the *lowest possible fare* to your destination at the time you want to fly. Mention the fact that you qualify for a senior discount, but be prepared to jump ship if you can get a better deal with a short-term sale rate or a supersaver fare—although sometimes your discount can cut these low fares even lower. Most airlines now offer sale fares during off-peak seasons, sometimes specifically for seniors. Watch for them because they are usually the cheapest way to go, although in most cases you can't deduct the regular senior discount from them.

■ Keep in mind that the restrictions you must fly by may not be worth the savings. Always examine the fees and conditions and decide whether you can live with them. There may be blackout periods around major holidays when you can't use your privileges, departures only on certain days or hours, restrictions on the season of the year, or stiff penalties for flight changes. In some plans, you must travel the entire distance on one airline even if connections are poor. It's not always easy to sort out the offers.

■ A 10 percent senior discount is obviously better than nothing, but on high-mileage trips you'll probably do much better through a senior club or with a coupon book.

■ Be prepared to present valid proof of age at the check-in counter. It's possible that your discount will not be honored if you don't have that proof with you, and you will have to pay the difference.

■ Virtually all airlines allow younger travel mates to fly with the same senior discount when you fly together for the entire trip.

■ Be flexible. To get the best fares when you use your senior discount, plan to fly at off-peak times, when the rest of the population isn't rushing off to faraway places. For example, noontime or late-night flights can be much cheaper than early-morning or dinnertime flights. Consider leaving on a different day—fares are often lower midweek or on Saturday. And obviously, flying off-season, when children aren't on vacation and there are no major holidays, may pay off with better prices.

■ Senior airline coupon books are still a very good buy today, although their prices have gone up over the years. With coupons, a 62-plus traveler can fly for much less than the regular coach fares for long trips and often less than sale fares. There are no senior coupons for travel to Europe, Asia, or other overseas destinations. Each coupon is good for a one-way trip, including connecting flights as long as you don't stop over at a connection point. Two coupons are generally required each way for Alaska and Hawaii.

■ The coupons have additional advantages, as we've mentioned above. With some exceptions, coupons for younger companions are not available, but you will get frequent-flyer mileage for the miles you fly. Each traveler requires a separate coupon book, which can't be shared with a spouse or anyone else, except on America West and US Airways, where seniors may use their coupons for children under 12 who accompany them. Eight-coupon books, now issued only by Continental and TWA, cost less per flight than four-coupon books.

■ After you've used the first coupon in your book, the remaining vouchers become nonrefundable, so don't buy the books unless you are sure you will use them all. Once issued, the coupons must be redeemed for tickets and reservations made within a year, but in most cases you have another year to travel because you can book flights 12 months ahead. You may buy the booklets from your travel agent or the airline.

■ Totally unused and unexpired coupon booklets are "fully refundable." However, two airlines now charge sizable service fees (up to $75) for the privilege. Most airlines also charge fees—from $50 to $75—to change your reservations once a ticket has been issued.

■ Remember that it costs the same for a few hundred miles as for several thousand, so don't waste your coupons on short trips. In other words, the longer the distance, the greater the savings. For shorter trips, you are probably better off with the 10 percent senior discount.

■ Book your flights as early as possible for the best fares and the most available seats. Seats for travel on senior coupons or senior discounts are limited and may not be reserved at all on some flights.

■ Four airlines—American, Continental, Delta, and United—now have clubs for seniors, all described on the following pages. Join one of them and you don't have to settle for a meager 10 percent discount, which is all most airlines offer seniors. They all provide benefits that include significant savings on airfares.

■ If you want to join a private airline VIP club so you can spend waiting time at airports in peace and comfort, complete with snacks and free drinks, copy machines, private telephones, luggage storage areas, and sometimes even showers, remember that you can buy a lifetime membership at age 62 for about half the regular fee from some airlines.

Now for some of the good deals awaiting you. Be advised that airfares and airline policies can change overnight—and often do—so always call the airline that interests you for an update.

U.S. AIRLINES

ALASKA AIRLINES

Fly on Alaska Airlines at 62-plus and you'll get 10 percent off almost all fares along with frequent-flyer credits. So will a traveling companion of any age.

For information: Call 800-426-0333.

AMERICA WEST AIRLINES

America West's Senior Saver Pack for travelers 62 and over is a packet of four one-way coupons good for coach travel on any of the airline's flights within the 48 contiguous United States and between those states and Vancouver, B.C. The coupons must be exchanged for tickets within a year.

An advantage of flying with this airline is that you may also use your coupons for one or two grandchildren between the ages of 2 and 12 when they travel with you. Also included in the packet are additional coupons offering 500 bonus miles plus savings on land packages and car rentals. A disadvantage is that travel days are limited. You may only fly from Monday noon through Thursday noon and all day Saturday, and there are many blackout dates when you can't use your coupons, mostly around major holidays. Reservations must be made at least 14 days in advance, although you may use your tickets to fly standby on valid travel days. You're entitled to frequent-flyer points for your miles.

If you don't purchase a coupon book, remember that you and a younger companion can count on a 10 percent discount on most coach fares. And remember to ask about the special senior fares offered occasionally.

For information: Call 800-235-9292.

AMERICAN AIRLINES

American Airlines has three good offers for passengers over 62. One is a 10 percent discount on any regular fare, even the lowest, for you and a traveling companion of any age.

Another is its Senior TrAAveler Coupon Books, which give you four coupons per book. Traded in for a ticket, each coupon is good for travel one way within a year in the contiguous 48 states and between the U.S. and Puerto Rico or the U.S. Virgin Islands. Flights to and from Hawaii require two coupons each way.

You may travel any day of the week with coupons, but you must exchange your coupons at least 14 days in advance of your flight or fly standby. There is no refund on the coupons and no change of itinerary on one-way tickets, although if you don't take your reserved flight, you may use the ticket for a standby seat to the same city. Seats are limited for coupon users, but you will get frequent-flyer credits for all the miles you fly. The same privileges apply to flights on American Eagle, AA's commuter airline affiliate.

AA is the first airline to allow you to book a flight using coupons that have expired before you have used them all up, but you must pay a service fee of $75. On the other hand, there is also a $75 fee when you turn in a totally unused coupon booklet for a refund.

The AActive American Traveler Club, launched in 1997, is yet another option for travelers over the age of 62. Members, who pay an annual fee of $40 for an individual or $70 for a senior and a companion of any age, may purchase coach tickets for both domestic and international travel at substantial discounts. Fares currently start at $98 for short hops on weekdays, and $20 more each way for weekends, so fare are less expensive for some short hops than the coupons' flat fee. Travel is blacked out around Thanksgiving and Christmas, and international travel, except to Canada, is available only Monday through Thursday.

Additional club benefits include discounts on vacations, car rentals, and cruises. Seats are limited and subject to availability. There is a 14-day advance reservation required, and you must stay over a Saturday night.

And, as with other airline clubs, enrollment may be closed periodically. If that's the case when you try to enroll, ask to be put on the waiting list.

For information: Call 800-433-7300 for reservations. For the Senior TrAAveler Coupon Books or the AActive American Traveler Club, call 800-421-5600.

AMERICAN TRANS AIR (ATA)

A low-fare airline based in the Midwest, ATA flies primarily to vacation destinations—Florida, Las Vegas, Los Angeles, Phoenix, San Francisco, Hawaii, and the Caribbean. It offers a 10 percent discount to passengers over the age of 62.

For information: Call 800-435-9282.

CONTINENTAL AIRLINES

Continental Airlines offers several excellent deals for senior travelers. First, there's the 10 percent discount on all fares, even the lowest, for you and a younger companion if you are at least 62. Simply ask for it and be ready to prove your age. You'll get mileage points.

The next choice is Freedom Trips, booklets of four or eight coupons, each to be traded for a one-way ticket on flights in the continental U.S., Canada, Mexico, the Caribbean, the Bahamas, Puerto Rico, and Bermuda. Two coupons are required for flights to Hawaii and Alaska. You must make reservations or changes at least 14 days in advance or travel standby. You may fly any day except during blackouts around major holidays—or fly standby—and you are entitled to frequent-flyer points for the miles you fly. You must redeem your coupons within a year after purchase, but you have another year to complete your travel.

Continental's newest seniors program is the Freedom Flight Club, also for travelers over 62. This is nice and simple: Members get a 15 to 20 percent discount anytime, anywhere, on all published fares including first-class and promotional sales, domestic or international. There are no seat limits or blackout dates, even during holidays. If a seat is available, you get it. Membership costs $75 a year for travel to all 50 states. International membership costs $125 a year and covers travel to all the states, plus Mexico, Canada, Central and South America, the Caribbean, and eight European cities.

For travel on this side of the Atlantic, the discount is 20 percent Monday through Thursday and on Saturday; and 15 percent on Friday and Sunday. For flights to Europe, the discount is 20 percent Monday through Thursday; and 15 percent on Friday, Saturday, and Sunday. Members are eligible for frequent-flyer credits but this plan does not accommodate a companion. As with the other airline clubs, enrollment is limited and may be closed periodically. Ask to be placed on the waiting list.

Bonus: A lifetime membership in Continental's President Club costs you, if you are 62, less than half of the regular adult fee.

And, if you are a member of AARP, you are also entitled to $25 to $50 savings on Continental Airlines' vacation packages.

For information: Call 800-523-3273. For Freedom Trips Coupon Books or Freedom Flight Club, call 800-441-1135.

DELTA AIRLINES

At age 62, you have some good options from Delta. The first is a 10 percent discount on virtually all published fares, even including most sale fares, for you and a travel partner for flights on Delta and Delta Connection within the continental U.S. and to Alaska, Hawaii, Puerto Rico, Canada, and the U.S. Virgin Islands. Seats are limited, so book early. Of course you'll be entitled to mileage points when you use the discount.

Your second choice from Delta is the Young at Heart Coupon program, which lets you purchase booklets of four coupons for a flat fee. The coupons must be traded within a year for tickets to any Delta destination in the continental United States, Puerto Rico, the U.S. Virgin Islands, or Canada, with two coupons required for flights to or from Alaska and Hawaii. You may fly any day of the week and you'll get frequent-flyer credits for your miles. Reservations and/or changes must be made at least 14 days before departure. Remember that only a limited number of seats are available for passengers using senior coupons, so plan ahead. Without reservations, you may travel standby any time.

Probably the best deal of all from Delta is its SkyWise Program, a club for travelers over 62. With limited membership, which means that enrollment is closed periodically, it provides access to special first-class and coach zone-fares to over 280 domestic destinations in the continental U.S., Alaska, and Hawaii, currently starting at $59 one way. It also includes travel discounts for vacation packages, hotels, rental cars, and cruises. Once you've joined for $40 a year, you may travel any day of the week, but seats are limited and may not be available on all flights. Round-trip tickets must be purchased 14 days in advance, and a Saturday-night stay is required. There's a maximum stay of 30 days but no blackout dates. Up to three companions, who get the same discounted fares when they travel with you, may be enrolled for $25 a year each.

Finally, members of AARP are entitled to savings of up to $50 per person on Delta's vacation packages all over the world.

For information: For reservations and Delta Young at Heart coupons, call 800-221-1212. For the Delta SkyWise Program, call 800-325-3750.

DELTA SHUTTLE

On shuttle flights between New York and Washington, D.C., or Boston, your fare is less than half the regular adult fare if you are at least 62 and can provide evidence of that fact before flight time. With this fare you may travel all day on Saturday and Sunday, or Monday through Friday between 10:30 A.M. and 2:30 P.M. or 7:30 P.M. and 9:30 P.M. No reservations are required. Just show up at the gate. You are eligible for frequent-flyer credits for your mileage.

You can also purchase a Delta Shuttle Flightpack Booklet for seniors that contains either four or eight coupons, each to be used for one-way travel, standby or with reservations, on the shuttle routes. With the coupons, you may fly at the same hours as above Monday through Friday or all day Saturday and Sunday. You'll be eligible for frequent-flyer miles. The coupon books may be purchased only in a shuttle city, although you may buy a voucher through your travel agent and trade it for the booklet when you arrive at the airport.

For information: Call 800-221-1212.

FRONTIER AIRLINES

If you are 62, you and a younger companion get a discount of 10 percent on this West Coast carrier.

For information: Call 800-432-1359.

HAWAIIAN AIRLINES

At age 60 or older, you may take advantage of this airline's senior fares on flights from the mainland to Honolulu and the South Pacific, as well as a special rate on the Hawaiian Island Pass which permits inter-island shuttle flights for 5 to 14 consecutive days.

For information: Call 800-367-5320.

HORIZON AIR

An airline that serves the Northwest corner of the country, Horizon Air gives the standard 10 percent discount on most fares to passengers 62 or older and their flying companions of any age.

For information: Call 800-547-9308.

KIWI INTERNATIONAL AIR LINES

Serving the East Coast as well as Las Vegas and San Juan, Kiwi takes 10 percent off your fare, except on special promotions, for you at age 62 and a travelmate. It also sells a Senior Discount Pack of six coupons good for one-way flights wherever the airline goes. Kiwi is the only airline that allows you and a companion traveling with you to use your coupons, which you will trade in for tickets. You must reserve within seven days of departure or fly standby any time. There are no fees for changing or canceling your flights, and no need to stay over Saturday night or to be concerned about blackouts when coupons can't be used.

For information: Call 800-JET-KIWI (800-538-5494).

MIDWAY AIRLINES

You and a travelmate of any age may take advantage of Midway's 10 percent senior discount if you are over 62. Or, at only 60, you may purchase the Senior Travel Coupon Booklet, a packet of four senior coupons redeemable for one-way travel to almost anywhere Midway or Midway Connection flies on the East Coast. Restrictions are minimal, with no minimum stay or Saturday-night stay required, but reservations must be made 14 days in advance. To take along a travel companion of any age, you can purchase a Companion Coupon Booklet for only $50 more than yours.

For information: Call 800-44-MIDWAY (800-446-4392).

MIDWEST EXPRESS AIRLINES

Ten percent is the discount on published fares for people over the age of 62 on Midwest Express, an airline that flies out of Milwaukee to many cities in the U.S.

For information: Call 800-452-2022.

NORTHWEST AIRLINES

You and a companion of any age get a senior discount of 10 percent, complete with frequent-flyer credits, on most of Northwest's published fares when you've attained the age of 62.

At the same age, you're also eligible to purchase NorthBest Senior Coupons, a booklet of four coupons, each good for a one-way flight within the lower 48 states and Canada and to Puerto Rico on Northwest or its affiliates. Two coupons are required each way to Hawaii and Alaska. For stopovers, an additional coupon is required. Reservations must be made 14 days in advance, but you may fly any time, any day, and collect mileage credits. Or you may fly standby any time. Coupons must be traded for tickets within a year.

Bonus: a lifetime membership in Northwest Airlines World Club will cost you only about a third of what it costs those who are younger.

For information: Call 800-225-2525.

RENO AIR

A low-fare airline, Reno Air serves 16 cities in the western U.S. and Canada plus Chicago and gives passengers over the age of 62 a discount of 10 percent on all published fares. If a competitive carrier offers a lower fare for seniors on the same route, Reno Air will match it.

For information: Call 800-RENO AIR (800-736-6247).

SOUTHWEST AIRLINES

On all flights every day of the year, travelers over 65 are offered special senior fares that vary from city to city and change frequently. Though reservations are required, advance purchase is not necessary, tickets are fully refundable, and you may buy one way only. Seats at the senior fares are limited, so reserve yours as early as possible. Check out promotional fares and Southwest's occasional Friends Fly Free program, which could be your best bet if you are traveling with a younger companion.

For information: Call 800-435-9792.

TWA (TRANS WORLD AIRLINES)

TWA reduces the fare by 10 percent for travelers 62 and over and companions of any age on almost all flights in the U.S. and Puerto Rico and some to Europe and the Middle East as well. Ask for the discount when you make reservations. You are entitled to frequent-flyer mileage.

The Senior Travel Pak is another alternative for travelers 62 or older. This gives you four or eight one-way domestic coupons at bargain prices (if you use them for long trips). Each coupon may be exchanged for a one-way ticket on flights in the mainland United States and Canada, plus Puerto Rico and Mexico. Two coupons are required each way for trips to or from Alaska and Hawaii. TWA's packets include discount certificates for a 20 percent reduction on a ticket to Europe, a $50 discount on a TWA Getaway Vacation package, and two upgrades on rental cars. You may travel any day of the week except around Thanksgiving and Christmas. Seats are limited so book yours early. Reservations must be made 14 days in advance, but you may travel standby anytime before your scheduled flight after you have traded your coupon for a ticket. You're entitled to mileage points.

TWA also issues four- or eight-coupon books for younger companions, at a $100 surcharge, to be used when you and a travelmate fly together. All of the coupons must be used by the same person. The discount certificate for travel to Europe is included.

One more benefit of age: a lifetime membership in TWA's Ambassador Club costs you at 62 less than half what it costs those who are younger.

For information: Call 800-221-2000.

UNITED AIRLINES

United has three programs that benefit mature travelers. The first is a 10 percent discount at age 62 on excursion fares for you and any traveling companion. The discount also applies to United Express, selected fares from regional carriers, and all fares on the Shuttle by United.

The next good deal is the Silver TravelPac program for passengers over 62, which offers packets of four coupons at a flat fee, each coupon good for a one-way ticket within mainland United States, and to San Juan or Canada. Two coupons are required each way to Hawaii or Alaska (except from Seattle). They may be used for flights any day of the week, although there are blackouts during holiday seasons, and you must trade them for tickets within a year of the purchase date. Reservations must be made at least 14 days in advance, but you may use the coupons to fly standby. You'll get mileage credits for the miles you fly. Remember, seats at discounted fares are always limited, so plan ahead.

UAL's third offer for mature travelers is Silver Wings Plus, a travel club which you may join at age 55 and become eligible for many benefits, such as discounts on hotels, rental cars, partner airlines, and cruises. Its low-cost fares for members are mileage-based for domestic travel and zone-based for international flights. Lifetime membership, which costs $225, includes bonus miles, three $50 certificates for flying on United anywhere and a $100 certificate for flying to Europe. A two-year membership for $75 includes three $25 certificates for flights and more certificates good for savings on everything from airfares to cruises, hotels, and car rentals. A companion of any age may join too.

And there's more. Members earn mileage points and upgrades and receive a quarterly newsletter. At age 62, they and a companion get the 10 percent senior discount on all published fares on United Airlines; on selected routes with international partners; and on some fares from regional carriers.

For information: Call 800-241-6522. For United Silver Wings Plus: 800-720-1765. For the Silver TravelPac: 800-633-6563.

SHUTTLE BY UNITED

Connecting 21 West Coast cities, the Shuttle by United offers the same 10 percent discount at age 62 for you and a younger companion.

For information: Call 800-SHUTTLE (800-748-8853).

US AIRWAYS

If you are over 62, you and a travel companion of any age can count on a 10 percent discount on all US Airways fares, including seasonal sales. The same discount applies to the US Airways Shuttle that flies between New York and Boston or Washington, D.C.

If you plan to fly frequently on this airline, consider the Golden Opportunities Coupon Booklet, a book of four coupons each good for a one-way ticket to any US Airways destination within the continental U.S., Canada, Mexico, the U.S. Virgin Islands, and Puerto Rico. Reservations must be made at least 14 days in advance, but you may travel standby anytime after a ticket has been issued. The coupons may be used for flights any day of the week but must be used within a year of purchase. You will get frequent-flyer points for your mileage. Totally unused and unexpired coupon booklets may be turned in for a refund for a $50 service fee.

Bonus: As many as two of your grandchildren, ages 2 through 11, may fly on your coupons if they make the trip with you.

For information: Call 800-428-4322.

VIRGIN ATLANTIC AIRWAYS

As soon as you turn 60, Virgin Atlantic gives you and a younger companion a 10 percent discount on all regular fares on all flights between the U.S. and London.

If you are a member of AARP, you—and your spouse or a companion of any age—can now save anywhere from 12 to 25 percent on all 45-day advance-purchase or higher economy fares to London, although not in addition to other promotional offers or discounts. When making a reservation, be sure you or your travel agent mentions the AARP offer, and be ready to present your membership card when you check in for your flight. The discounts are not applicable for a few weeks around Easter and Christmas/New Year's holidays. As a member, you can also save $50 to $100 on the airline's vacation packages, except on promotional sales, to Great Britain and other European destinations.

For information: Call 800-862-8621 for reservations. Call 888-YES-VIRGIN (888-937-8474) for vacation packages.

GOOD DEALS ON CANADIAN AIRLINES

AIR CANADA

If you are over 60, you and any traveling companion are eligible for a 10 percent reduction on all fares, including sale fares, for flights in Canada and the U.S., including Florida, and on trips between Canada and the U.K. and the Caribbean. You'll get mileage credits as well.

For information: Call 800-776-3000 in the U.S., 800-361-8620 in Canada.

CANADIAN AIRLINES INTERNATIONAL

The Canadian Golden Discount for passengers 60 or over gives you and a traveling companion of any age a 10 percent reduction on most fares on Canadian Airlines and all of its partners to destinations in Canada and the continental U.S., Mexico, and the U.K., and on certain fares to Hawaii. You get frequent-flyer credits for your mileage, and there are no special restrictions on time, day, or season.

For information: Call 800-426-7000 in the U.S.; 800-665-1177 in Canada.

GOOD DEALS ON FOREIGN AIRLINES

Again, always inquire about special senior discounts when you book a flight, even if you don't see them listed here. Airlines change their policies with very little notice. Your travel agent can provide current information. Remember, too, that seasonal promotional fares available to all travelers can often be much lower than the fare you can get with your senior discount, so do your homework before committing yourself.

EURAIR

If you plan to fly between cities in Europe, you may beat the usual high cost of airfares by buying a Europe Flight Pass from EurAir. Sold in packets of three or more coupons, each coupon currently costs $90 and is valid on 11 domestic airlines for a nonstop flight between any two cities in the system. Reservations can be made before leaving the U.S. or when you need them while traveling in Europe. There is no senior discount, however.
For information: Call 888-387-2479.

AEROLINEAS ARGENTINAS

On this airline, passengers over the age of 60 and a companion of any age are offered a 10 percent discount on posted fares for flights originating in the United States to any of its South American destinations.
For information: Call 800-333-0276.

AEROLITORAL

A commuter airline operated by Aeromexico that flies from several cities in the U.S. Southwest to Mexico, Aerolitoral offers a 10 percent discount on its regular economy fares to passengers over 62.
For information: Call 800-237-7113.

AEROMEXICO

It's 10 percent off the regular first-class or tourist fares every day on all Aeromexico routes, domestic and international, out of U.S. gateways if you are over 62.
For information: Call 800-237-6639.

AIR FRANCE

If you're 62, a 10 percent discount is yours on most Air France flights—whether first class, business, or economy—between U.S. and Canadian gateway cities and destinations in Europe. Exceptions are some weekend and short-term promotional fares. Your younger traveling companion gets the discount too.

You are eligible for the same discount on domestic flights within France when you fly Air France to Europe, if your travel originates in the U.S. or Canada.
For information: Call 800-237-2747.

AIR JAMAICA

Fly to Jamaica in the off-peak season, which usually means spring and fall, and you can take advantage of Air Jamaica's

20 percent discount offered to passengers over the age of 60 on flights between the U.S. and Jamaica. Fly in a peak period and you'll get a 10 percent discount. Either way, a younger traveling companion gets the same discount you do. You must travel first class or economy on Tuesdays, Wednesdays, or Thursdays, plus Saturdays on flights between Miami or Fort Lauderdale and Jamaica. If you cancel your trip after ticketing, you will be charged a $25 service fee.

For information: Call 800-523-5585.

ALITALIA

When you fly on Alitalia to its European destinations or Egypt, you qualify for a 10 percent discount when you are 62, as does a younger traveling companion. When you travel on an advance-purchase fare via Alitalia from the U.S. to Israel, you will get a 15 percent discount off standard fares if you are 60. So will your spouse if he or she accompanies you and is at least 55.

On certain domestic flights within Italy, seniors over 65 are offered special discounted Terza Eta (Third Age) fares. Be sure to ask for them.

For information: 800-223-5730.

BRITISH AIRWAYS

You qualify at age 60 for a 10 percent discount for yourself and a traveling companion when you book an advance-purchase economy-class flight on British Airways from its U.S. gateway cities to the U.K., Europe, or other parts of the world. Not only that, but the fees are waived for canceling or changing your reservations before you depart. If you make a change to your return flight, it will cost you only $50, although it costs younger people $150 to do the same.

However, always be sure to check out the 90-day advance-purchase fares and any ongoing promotional sales because these may save you more money than the senior discount.

For information: Call 800-AIRWAYS.

BWIA INTERNATIONAL AIRLINES

A 10 percent discount is yours if you are at least 62 years old. A younger companion may fly with you at the same fare.

For information: Call 800-327-7401.

CAYMAN AIRWAYS

This small airline that flies from Miami, Tampa, Orlando, or Houston to the Cayman Islands will take 10 percent off most fares if you are 62.

For information: 800-422-9626.

EL AL ISRAEL AIRLINES

Travelers over the age of 60 and their spouses over 55 are entitled to El Al's senior fare, which gives you a discount of about 15 percent off the regular Apex fare between the U.S. and Israel. You may stay for up to two months, a 14-day advance purchase is required, and there is a $50 fee for changing your return flight.

But, before accepting this deal, check out the cheaper superapex fare with its maximum stay of 45 days. It may work out better for you, as may the Early Bird Fare that is offered a couple of times a year. And don't forget to look into El Al's economical Israel Milk and Honey Vacation packages, available only with a round-trip ticket from the U.S. to Tel Aviv.

Traveling with your grandchildren? If they are under 12, the first one flies at 25 percent off, the second at 50 percent off, and the third at 75 percent off.

For information: Call 800-223-6700. For El Al packages, call 800-352-5786.

FINNAIR

On flights between gateway cities in the U.S. and Canada and Helsinki, Finland, you will get a 10 percent reduction off the regular economy fares if you are 65 years old or more. Travel companions of any age get the same discount. You'll get an even better discount—a whopping 70 to 75 percent—on Finnair's domestic flights in Finland. You must be 65 and pay for your tickets within three days of booking your flight.

For information: Call 800-950-5000.

IBERIA AIRLINES OF SPAIN

Iberia gives you 10 percent off regular published fares for transatlantic flights originating in North America, except on promotional sales. You must have reached 62 to get the privilege, but you may take a younger companion who pays the same fare.

For information: Call 800-772-4642.

KLM ROYAL DUTCH AIRLINES

KLM's discount for people over the age of 62 is 10 percent on all nonpromotional fares between the U.S. and its European destinations. Flying on KLM to Paris from the U.S., your discount is even better—30 percent. A companion of any age is entitled to the same reduction in fare if you travel together for the entire journey. On flights within Europe from Amsterdam, you can get a 10 percent discount on fares if you are over 60.

For information: Call 800-374-7747.

LACSA AIRLINES

Flying from the U.S. to many destinations in Central and South America, Costa Rica's Lacsa Airlines gives travelers over 55 departing from Miami or Orlando a special senior rate. From other gateway cities—New Orleans or San Francisco—the discount is 10 percent off the fares at 55. From New York or Los Angeles, you must be 62 to qualify for the same reduction.

For information: Call 800-225-2272.

LUFTHANSA

After you have turned 60, you get 10 percent off most Lufthansa fares across the Atlantic Ocean to European destinations for you and a travelmate over the age of 18. The same reduction applies to domestic flights inside the German borders.

For information: Call 800-645-3880.

MARTINAIR HOLLAND

Martinair flies from nine North American gateway cities to Amsterdam and other European destinations. To travelers over 60 and a younger companion it offers a 10 percent discount on excursion fares for one-month, two-month, or six-month stays abroad.

For information: Call 800-MARTINAIR (800-627-8462).

MEXICANA AIRLINES

A senior discount of 10 percent applies to most Mexicana international flights between gateway cities in the U.S. or Canada and Mexico. You must be 62, but your traveling companion may be younger and fly at the same fare.

For information: Call 800-531-7921.

OLYMPIC AIRWAYS

The national airline of Greece, Olympic Airways gives passengers over the age of 62 and their younger travelmates a 10 percent discount on most flights from its gateway cities of Boston and New York to Athens and other European destinations. Older Canadians departing from Montreal or Toronto also get a special rate. On domestic flights within Greece, passengers over 60 pay only 80 percent of the regular adult fare, so remember to ask about it.

For information: Call 800-223-1226 (in the New York area, call 212-838-3600).

SABENA BELGIAN WORLD AIRLINES

At 62, you are entitled to a 10 percent discount on all fares except promotional packages from the United States to Belgium and via Brussels to other Sabena destinations in Europe. For an even better deal, look into Sabena's Euro-starters, low-cost packages. Available all year, their lowest fares are offered November through March. In addition, Sabena offers special senior fares to travelers over 60 and spouses over 55 on round-trip flights to Israel. You must stay a minimum of six days and a maximum of two months and book a week in advance. Bonus: one free stopover in the United States and another in Europe on your way to or from Tel Aviv.

For information: Call 800-955-2000.

SAS (SCANDINAVIAN AIRLINES SYSTEM)

On flights across the Atlantic from gateway cities in the United States to Scandinavia or European destinations, passengers over 62 get a 10 percent discount on most fares.

In addition, SAS gives those over 65 special senior fares on domestic flights within Norway on tickets sold in the U.S. If you are 67 and purchase tickets while in Norway, you'll get an even better deal—half-fare—on the same flights.

On domestic flights within Denmark, the discount is 20 percent on certain fares, depending on the route, again if you're 65.

Within Sweden, SAS also offers special senior fares, which vary according to the route, to passengers over 65.

For information: Call 800-221-2350.

SWISSAIR

Swissair offers two good options to travelers over the age of 62 (in Canada, 60) and their younger traveling companions. One is a 10 percent discount on almost all published fares on flights on Swissair or any of its partners from

10 U.S. and Canadian gateway cities to destinations in Europe. Yours for the asking, it is available on flights all year round and every day of the week.
For information: Call 800-221-4750.

TAP AIR PORTUGAL

Your discount from this airline if you are at least 62 is 10 percent off almost any fare on flights between the United States and Portugal, Madeira, and the Azores. The discount applies to a younger flying partner as well. Watch for TAP's occasional special packages for seniors.
For information: Call 800-221-7370.

VARIG BRAZILIAN AIRLINES

On flights originating in the U.S. and flying to Rio de Janeiro or Sao Paulo, Varig gives passengers over the age of 62 a 10 percent discount on all fares.
For information: Call 800-468-2744.

8

Beating the Costs
of Car Rentals

Never rent a car without getting a discount or a special promotional rate. Almost all car-rental agencies in the United States and Canada give them to all manner of customers, including those who belong to over-50 organizations (see Chapter 19) or have reached a certain birthday. The discount that's coming to you as a senior member of society can save you some money, although short-term sales will almost always save you more. Refer to the membership material sent by the group to which you belong for information about your discount privileges.

It's almost impossible to sort out the confusing choices of rates, discounts, and add-on fees from the rental companies. To save money, you must shop around, compare costs, and make many decisions that can raise or lower your bill. And then make sure you get the senior discount for renters over 50. It may not amount to much, but it will help a little.

But, first, keep in mind:

■ Car-rental agents may not always volunteer information about senior discounts or special sales, so always ask for it when you reserve your car.

■ Don't settle for a senior discount or senior rate too hastily without investigating the possibility of an even better deal. Shop around yourself or ask your travel agent to find the *lowest available rate or package* at the time you are going to travel, and don't forget to ask about airport fees, taxes, and other extra charges. Senior discounts are usually given on the full published rental rate. So special promotional rates—in other words, sales—or even weekend rates are almost always better, sometimes much better. On the other hand, if you can get the senior discount *on top of the lowest posted rate*, regular or promotional, that's the deal you want. Thrifty, for example, guarantees a 10 percent discount off the lowest available rate.

■ Book your car as far in advance as you can, especially if you are traveling during a holiday season. Generally, the later you book the more expensive it will be and the less likely you are to get the car you want. If closer to departure you find a better rate that suits your needs, you can rebook it.

■ Remember that weekly and weekend rates are less expensive than daily rates.

■ Read newspapers and magazines—especially those targeting over-50s. Look for ads for seasonal sales and clip out "value-added coupons" for additional discounts, cash savings, or upgrades. Sometimes you'll also get coupons in the mail from clubs, associations, frequent-flyer programs, and credit-card companies. Your travel agent may have some to offer too.

■ If you have access to the Internet, check the rental agencies' websites for special deals and last-minute offers.

■ Before driving away in your rented car, inspect it for dents, scratches, or other damage. If you find any, ask the agent to sign a statement on the condition of the car and attach it to your rental agreement. That way, you won't be in danger of being charged for the damage upon your return.

■ Ask if there is an additional-driver fee and don't sign up for it if you don't need it. If your spouse will be a second driver, rent from a company that allows a husband or wife to drive at no extra cost.

■ When you reserve a car, always ask for a confirmation number. When you pick up your car, verify the discount or special rate *before* signing the agreement and ask if a better rate has become available since you booked.

■ When you call to ask about rates or reservations, always be armed with your organization's ID number and your own membership card for reference. Present them again at the rental counter when you pick up your car and be sure to confirm your rate before signing the agreement.

■ Special savings may not be available at every location, so remember to check them out every time you make a reservation.

■ Don't purchase insurance you don't need. Review your personal auto insurance coverage and credit-card policy to determine if you require the optional loss/damage coverage offered by the rental companies. Your homeowner's policy may cover your personal belongings on the road.

■ If you want to rent a car in Europe, be sure to ask the rental agency if it imposes age restrictions on drivers. These vary by country and agency. One agency, for example, denies rentals to people over 65 in Greece and Northern Ireland, or over 75 in Ireland and Israel. In the United Kingdom and Ireland, most agencies will not rent a car to a driver over 75. So make your age clear when you make your reservation. Shop around, and also consider leasing a car, in which case age may not be an issue.

■ If you are traveling outside the United States, don't wait until you arrive at your destination to arrange a rental. Book it here before you go because renting abroad is much more expensive. Remember to request your senior discount. Check your insurance carrier and credit-card company to be sure you are covered overseas. Most personal automobile insurance covers you only for driving in the U.S. and may not cover certain types of vehicles.

■ If you can drive a stick shift, you can cut the cost of a rental significantly. In other countries, automatic transmissions are not readily available and when they are, they are much more expensive.

ADVANTAGE RENT-A-CAR

This agency, with about 100 locations in seven western states, gives members of AARP a discount of 5 percent on all retail rental rates.

For information: Call 800-777-5500.

ALAMO RENT A CAR

Alamo's Experienced Driver Discount is available to anyone over the age of 50. On rentals in the U.S., it takes 10 per-

cent off the regular weekly rates and 3 percent off regular daily rates. At European locations, including the U.K., the reduction is 15 percent on both weekly and daily retail rates. To get the discount, you must specifically request it when you book your car at least 24 hours in advance.
For information: Call 800-GO-ALAMO (800-462-5266).

AVIS RENT-A-CAR

What you get from Avis if you are a member of AARP or CARP is a discount ranging from 5 to 20 percent on the lowest available rate, depending on availability and enhanced insurance coverage. All rates include unlimited free mileage at participating locations. Watch the coupon ads in over-50 publications that give members more savings or upgrades in addition to the discount.
For information: Call 800-331-1800.

BUDGET RENT-A-CAR

If you are over 50 and a member of a senior organization such as AARP, you are entitled to a discount of 10 percent off Budget's standard rental rates worldwide.
For information: Call 800-527-0700.

DOLLAR RENT A CAR

The Silver Dollar Club for renters over the age of 50 gives you a discount of at least 4 percent—and sometimes as much as 25 percent—off the regular retail rates. To be sure to get it, however, you must make an advance reservation, request the special rate, and mention the customer discount number SR1136.
For information: Call 800-800-4000. For information

about the club and to request value-added senior coupons, call 888-876-6873.

ENTERPRISE RENT-A-CAR

Enterprise specializes in renting vehicles in neighborhoods, placing its locations "where people live and work," rather than in airports and big cities. It offers a discount of 5 percent off the regular rental rates to members of AARP and CARP.

For information: Call 800-RENT-A-CAR (800-736-8222).

HERTZ CAR RENTAL

Members of several senior organizations such as AARP are entitled to savings worldwide when they rent from Hertz, the amount ranging from 5 percent to 15 percent depending on availability and type of rate. Unlimited mileage is included, as is enhanced insurance coverage for AARP members. Remember to clip the coupons in the AARP publications that give members more savings or upgrades at Hertz in addition to the discount.

For information: Call 800-654-2200.

KEMWEL HOLIDAY AUTOS

With more than 4,000 locations in over 60 countries, KHA operates mainly in Europe but also rents cars to consumers in many cities in the U.S., mainly in California, Florida, and Texas. Kemwel will give you a 5 percent discount off the regular rates anywhere in the world if you are age 60 or older.

For information: Call 800-678-0678.

NATIONAL CAR RENTAL

Members of AARP and CARP get discounts of 5 to 20 percent on the lowest quoted rates at National's locations in the U.S. and Canada, and 5 to 25 percent off published rates at international locations, plus unlimited mileage and enhanced insurance coverage. There are also coupons in the AARP publications that give members additional savings or upgrades on top of the discount at this agency.
For information: Call 800-227-7368.

PAYLESS CAR RENTAL

Travelers 50 and over get a straightforward 5 percent discount off the lowest applicable rate, including promotional sales, when they've joined the free Nifty Fifty Program.
For information: Call 800-PAYLESS (800-729-5377).

THRIFTY CAR RENTAL

Now here's a really good deal. If you are over 55, Thrifty guarantees you a 10 percent discount off its rates—including special promotional rates—at all of its locations all over the world. When you make a reservation, be sure to ask for that moment's very best rate for the car you want, then make sure you get the additional 10 percent off. You must show identification at the counter when you pick up your car.
For information: Call 800-367-2277.

U-SAVE AUTO RENTAL OF AMERICA

U-Save Auto Rental, with about 400 locations in the U.S. and Canada, provides vehicles to consumers and businesses as needed in local neighborhoods. Many of its locations offer discounts of 5 to 10 percent off the regular rates to older customers, so ask when you call for a car. And ask, too, if there are special rates at the moment that will save you more.

For information: Call 800-438-2300.

9

Saving a Bundle on Trains, Buses, and Boats in North America

etting around town, especially in a city where driving is not a practical option, probably means depending on public transportation to get you from hither to yon. Remember that, once you reach a particular birthday—in most cases, your 60th or 65th—you can take advantage of some good senior markdowns on trains, buses, subways and, in some places, even taxis. All you usually need is a Medicare card, a Senior ID card, or your driver's license to play this game, which usually reduces fares by half. Although you may find it uncomfortable at first to pull out that card and flash it at the bus driver or ticket agent, it soon becomes very easy. Do it and you'll realize some nice savings.

And don't fail to take advantage of the bargains available to seniors on long-distance rail, bus, and boat travel as well.

RIDING THE RAILS

Probably every commuter railroad in the United States and Canada gives older riders a break, although you may have to do your traveling during off-peak periods when the trains are not filled with go-getters rushing to and from their offices. Ask for your discount when you purchase your ticket.

As for serious long-distance travel, many mature travelers are addicted to the railroads, finding riding the rails a leisurely, relaxed, romantic, comfortable, economical, and satisfying way to make miles while enjoying the scenery.

So many passes and discounts on railroads are available to travelers heading for other parts of the country that sorting them out becomes confusing. But, once you do, they will help stretch your dollars while you cover a lot of ground.

See Chapter 4 for the best deals on transportation in foreign countries for travelers of a certain age.

AMTRAK

To accommodate senior travelers, Amtrak offers a 15 percent discount on the lowest available coach fares, including All Aboard America Passes, and on some Canadian routes, every day of the week to anyone over 62. The discount is also available on the Metroliner Service on Saturdays and Sundays but does not apply to the North America Rail Pass, Auto Train, or sleeping accommodations. Consider taking your grandchildren with you because, up to age 15, they ride at 50 percent of the regular adult fare.

The lowest coach fares often sell out quickly, so try

to book early. Not all fares are available on every train and some have restrictions that may not suit your plans, which means you should always ask questions before you buy.

For information: Amtrak, 800-USA-RAIL (800-872-7245).

ALASKA RAILROAD

Passengers over 65 are entitled to a 25 percent reduction in weekend fares during the winter months—late September through mid-May—between Anchorage and Fairbanks and anywhere in between. Remember to take food and drink with you. There's no food service on the train for this 12-hour journey.

For information: Alaska Railroad, 800-544-0552.

VIA RAIL CANADA

The government-owned Canadian passenger railroad offers you, at age 60, 10 percent off the regular coach fare every day of the year with no restrictions. Add this 10 percent to the 40 percent reduction on off-peak travel, available to all ages and applicable any day of the week except Friday and Sunday, and you end up with tickets that are half price. Tickets at the off-peak rate must be purchased at least five or seven days in advance. However, the number of seats sold at this rate is limited, so plan ahead and buy your tickets as early as possible.

When you reach the age of 60, you are also eligible to buy a Canrailpass at a 10 percent discount. The pass allows you to travel for any 12 days during a 30-day period anywhere on Via Rail's transcontinental system. You may board and deboard the train as many times as you wish, stopping wherever you like along the way after reserving your space for your segments.

For information: Via Rail Canada, PO Box 8116, Station A, Montreal, QE H3C 3N3. Book through Amtrak or a U.S. travel agent.

GOING BY BUS

Never, never board a bus without asking the driver whether there's a senior discount, because even the smallest bus lines in the tiniest communities (and the largest—New York City, for example) in this country and abroad give seniors a break, usually half fare at age 60 or 65. In Europe, your senior rail pass is often valid on major motorcoach lines as well, so always be sure to ask.

GREYHOUND BUS LINES

When Greyhound does the driving, you are entitled to a 10 percent reduction on any last-minute "walk up" fares if you have passed your 55th birthday. Be prepared to show a photo ID with proof of age. It pays to plan ahead, however, because advance-purchase fares are usually a much better deal than what you'll get with your senior discount, and sometimes there are special sales that are even better than those. For example, the periodic Friends Ride Free promotion that lets you ride at half price if you travel with someone else on the seasonal 21-day advance-purchase fares. By the way, seniors also get a 10 percent discount on Greyhound's Ameripass, which gives you unlimited travel for 7, 15, or 30 days to any U.S. destinations.

For information: Call your local Greyhound reservation office or 800-231-2222.

GREYHOUND CANADA

Here you'll get 10 percent off all regular fares, any day of the week, all year around, if you are a traveler over 60 with a valid ID. What's more, if you're accompanied by a younger companion and buy your tickets seven days in advance, the companion travels for half the regular adult fare. The 10 percent discount also applies to the Canadapass, which is good for unlimited travel wherever Greyhound goes for specified numbers of days.

For information: Greyhound Canada, 800-661-8747 or 403-265-9111.

GRAY LINE WORLDWIDE

Gray Line is an association of 150 small, independent sight-seeing-tour companies serving about 200 destinations on six continents. Most of them give a discount of 10 percent on sight-seeing tours, half- or full-day, to members of AARP who purchase tour tickets directly from Gray Line and present a valid membership card. Some Gray Line companies also give discounts to nonmembers if they are age 55 or 60, so be sure to inquire before signing up for a tour.

For information: Call the Gray Line Worldwide office in your area or the corporate headquarters at 303-433-9800.

ONTARIO NORTHLAND

This passenger railroad serving northeastern Ontario gives travelers over the age of 60 a 10 percent fare reduction any day of the year on the Northlander train running between Toronto and Cochrane. On the Polar Bear Express, a summer excursion line between Cochrane and Moosonee, the discount is about 25 percent.

SEE THE SIGHTS AT HALF PRICE

Don't visit Boston, New York, Philadelphia, San Francisco, or Seattle without a CityPass in your pocket. A booklet of admission tickets (good for seven to nine days) to six of each city's most popular cultural and entertainment attractions, the CityPass is a great buy. Prices for the passes vary from city to city but are always at least 50 percent less than the cost of the total admission to all of the included attractions. Not only that, but they provide actual tickets, not vouchers or coupons, so you won't have to wait in ticket lines. And they are discounted for sightseers over the age of 65. For example, in New York, the CityPass costs $26.75 per adult at this writing but only $18 for seniors. The San Francisco pass costs $27.75 per adult, $19.75 for seniors. Available at participating attractions and city information centers, or via the Internet.

For information: Call 707-256-0490 for general information. At the website www.citypass.net, you can buy a CityPass in advance for any of the five cities (more soon to be added) with a credit card.

For information: Ontario Northland, 555 Oak St. East, North Bay, ON P1B 8L3; 800-268-9281 or 705-472-4500.

TRENTWAY WAGAR

This bus line, which serves southwest Ontario and the Niagara Peninsula and runs between Toronto and Montreal, offers discounts up to 25 percent to passengers over the age of 60. In cooperation with Greyhound (U.S.), it also offers through service to Boston, New York, Washington, and Chicago.

For information: Trentway Wagar, 791 Webber Ave., Peterborough ON K9J 7A5; 800-461-7661 or 705-748-6411.

VOYAGEUR COLONIAL LTD.

This Canadian motorcoach line's Club 60 offers you a discount of 25 percent on all regular one-way bus fares throughout the provinces of Quebec and Ontario, without prior reservations, seven days a week. Simply present proof of your age when you buy your tickets.
For information: Voyageur Colonial Ltd.; 514-842-2281 in Montreal; 613-238-5900 in Ottawa.

GOING BY BOAT
ALASKA MARINE HIGHWAY

Traveling on the Alaska Marine Highway in the off-season is a bargain for foot passengers 65 and older. Between October and April, you sail for half the regular adult fare within Alaskan waters. The discount does not apply to vehicle or cabin space. Sometimes in the summer, too, there are half fares for seniors on several of the smaller vessels. The message is: always ask if a senior rate is available.
For information: Alaska Marine Highway, 800-642-0066.

TOURING BY BOAT, RAIL, BUS
THE ALASKAPASS

With an AlaskaPass, you may travel on many kinds of surface transportation in Alaska and the Yukon Territory for a specified number of days, using gateways in British Columbia and the state of Washington. One set discounted price allows unlimited travel on participating ferries, buses, and trains. These include the Alaska Marine Highway ferries, the Alaskan Express Motorcoaches, the Alaska Railroad, Alaska Direct Bus Line, B.C. Rail, Laidlaw Coach

Lines, Gray Lines of Seattle, Greyhound Canada, and Norline Coaches (Yukon). You plan your own itinerary, make your own reservations, and pay for your transportation with the pass, using, if you like, suggested itineraries. If you are planning a trip, you may wish to send for the *Alaska-Pass Handbook* ($5), which provides itineraries, lodging information, schedules, and general information for independent travelers.

The Rail to Sail Tour offered by AlaskaPass first takes you by train from Seattle to Vancouver, B.C., then along the coast to Prince George. From here you travel to Prince Rupert, staying overnight in each place before you depart on BC Ferries for an overnight cruise through the Inside Passage to Port Hardy. Now you go by motorcoach to Victoria and finish with a ferry back to Seattle. Tours and most meals are included. If you're over 60, you get $20 deducted from the cost.

For information: Call AlaskaPass, 800-248-7598. For the AlaskaPass Handbook, send $5 (U.S. or Canadian, postpaid) to AlaskaPass, PO Box 351, Vashon, WA 98070.

10

Hotels and Motels: Get Your Over-50 Markdowns

Now that you're past 50, you'll never have to pay full price for a hotel room again. Across the United States and Canada, and often in the rest of the world today, virtually all lodging chains and most individual establishments go out of their way to give you a break on room rates.

You don't even have to wait until you're eligible for Social Security to cash in on your maturity because most hotels, inns, and motels offer discounts to you at age 50, usually requiring only proof of age or membership in a senior organization. Often the best discounts, sometimes as high as 50 percent, however, are reserved at some hotel chains for members of their own senior travel clubs. Some cost little or nothing to join; others charge a yearly fee.

What all this means is that you should *never* make a lodging reservation without making sure you are getting a special rate—a senior discount of at least 10 percent or an even better deal, such as a promotional sale or weekend rate that is lower. Always ask for the senior discount, whether or not one is posted or mentioned in the hotel's literature, and then ask if a better rate is available.

The only bad news is that senior hotel discounts aren't as generous as they were a few years ago and restrictions have increased, for the simple reason that travel is booming and more people are turning 50 than ever before. Even so, dozens of hotel chains and thousands of individual hotels continue to use price incentives to attract over-50 travelers. It makes sense to take advantage of them whenever you can.

But, first, keep in mind:

If you want to take advantage of the privileges coming to you because of your age, you must do some advance research and planning with your travel agent or on your own.

- In this rapidly changing world, rates and policies can be altered in a flash, so an update is always advisable.
- Information about discounts is seldom volunteered. In most cases, you must arrange for discounts when you make your reservations and confirm them again when you check in. Do not wait until you're settling your bill because then it may be too late. Some hotels and motels require that you make advance reservations to get their discounts. "Advance" may mean a considerable period of time such as three weeks, but it may also mean only a week, a day, or even a few hours. Check it out before making your plans.

■ Although many senior discounts are available every day of the year, some are subject to "space availability." This means it may be pretty hard to get them when you want to travel because only a limited number of rooms may be reserved for special rates. If these are already booked (or are expected to be booked), you won't get your discount. And some hotels have "blackout" dates during special events or holiday periods when the discount is not valid. So always book early, ask for your discount privileges, and try to be flexible on your dates in order to take advantage of them. Your best bets for space are usually weekends in large cities, weekdays at resorts, and non–holiday seasons.

■ It's quite possible that a special promotional rate, especially off-peak or on weekends, may save you more money than your senior discount. Many hotels, particularly in big cities and warm climates, cut their prices drastically in the summer, for example. Others that cater mostly to businesspeople during the week try to encourage weekend traffic by offering bargain rates if you stay over a Saturday night. Resorts are often eager to fill their rooms on weekdays. So always investigate all the possibilities before you get too enthusiastic about using your hard-earned senior discount, and remember to ask for the *lowest available rate*.

■ There are several chains of no-frills budget motels that may not offer discounts or too much in the way of amenities but do charge very low room rates and tend to be located along the most-traveled routes.

■ In some cases, not every hotel or inn in a chain will offer the discount. Those that do are called "participating" hotels/motels. Make sure the one you are planning to visit is participating in the senior plan.

- In addition to the chains, many independent hotels and inns are eager for your business and offer special reduced rates. Always *ask* before making a reservation. Your travel agent should be able to help you with this.
- Some hotel restaurants will give you a discount too, sometimes whether or not you are a registered guest.
- By the way, your discount usually applies only to the regular rates and, in most cases, will not be given on top of other special discounts. One discount is all you get.

AMERIHOST INN

At these motels concentrated in the Midwest, there's a senior discount of 10 percent on the rates.
For information: Call 800-434-5800.

AMERISUITES

This nationwide chain of all-suite accommodations designed for extended stays offers members of AARP and CARP a 10 percent discount off the regular rates.
For information: Call 800-833-1516.

ASTON HOTELS & RESORTS

Aston's Sun Club gives travelers 50 and older—and their roommates—25 percent per night off room rates at its hotels and condominium resorts, budget to luxury, on Hawaii's four major islands, plus special rates on car rentals and a seventh night free. Ask for these privileges when you make your reservations and pick up a coupon book of discounts when you check in. Sun Club rooms are limited, so reserve early.

For information: Call 800-922-7866.

BEST INNS

At these inexpensive inns mainly in the Midwest and South, anyone over 50 gets 10 percent off the regular rates.

For information: Call 800-237-8466.

BEST WESTERN INTERNATIONAL

Just show your AARP or CARP membership card or prove you're over 55, and you will get at least a 10 percent savings on regular rates every day of the year at every one of the 3,800 Best Westerns in the world. You will also be entitled to at least two special amenities at each hotel. These may include a complimentary continental breakfast, free local phone calls, a free newspaper, a room upgrade, late checkout, or other local offerings that may change by the season.

For information: Call 800-528-1234.

BUDGET HOST INNS

A network of about 180 affiliated, mostly family-owned economy inns in 37 states and Canada, most Budget Host Inns offer senior discounts—usually 10 percent off the regular rates—that vary by location. Call the toll-free reservation number and you will be transferred directly to the front desk of the inn. Ask as many questions as you like about the accommodations, facilities, rates, discounts, and directions to the property.

For information: Call 800-283-4678.

BUDGETEL INNS

At these inexpensive motels located mainly in the South and Midwest, you will get up to 10 percent off just for being over 55. You will get it at 50 if you are a member of AARP.
For information: Call 800-428-3438.

CAMBERLEY HOTELS

Most of these charming upscale hotels, some of them landmark buildings, give AARP members 10 percent off the standard room rates.
For information: Call 800-555-8000.

CANADIAN PACIFIC HOTELS & RESORTS

These grand hotels and resorts throughout Canada give a 30 percent discount on regular room rates, subject to availability, to members of AARP and CARP. Some hotels offer 25 percent off the rate to other guests over 65.

Also, be sure to check out the special off-peak packages designed for older travelers at many Canadian Pacific hotels. For example: the Seniors Spring Fling, the Seniors Fall Getaway, the Sixty-Something room rate, and the Second Honeymoon.
For information: Call 800-441-1414.

CASTLE RESORTS & HOTELS

The Castle Group, with 21 hotels and resort condominiums on the five Hawaiian islands and Saipan, offers its Castle Advantage Program that gives you and your party a really good deal if you are at least 50 years old. You get a discount of 25 percent or more on the regular room rates, an air-conditioned compact car with unlimited mileage for $29

AMERICAN EXPRESS SENIOR CARD

A charge card especially for retirees, the Senior Member Card from American Express provides a program of benefits and services. It gives you the usual American Express charge privileges and customer services, plus a quarterly newsletter and savings on travel, shopping, and dining. The Senior Global Assist Hotline is available 24 hours a day. Through it, members can get medical or legal referrals, get rush replacements on prescriptions and eyeglasses, or send emergency messages to family or friends. The Pharmacist on Call Hotline, open from 8 A.M. until 1 A.M. seven days a week, puts you in touch with a pharmacist who answers questions about medications. If you are over 62, you pay a reduced annual membership fee of $35 for the standard Senior Member Card or $55 for a Gold Senior Member Card.

For information: Call 800-THE CARD (800-843-2273).

a day, and special rates at nearby golf courses. Also watch for special senior packages that are even better.

For information: Call 800-367-5004.

CHOICE HOTELS INTERNATIONAL

Choice Hotels is an international group of more than 4,000 inns in 33 countries with brand names that include Clarion, Comfort, Quality, Sleep, Econo Lodge, MainStay Suites, and Rodeway. All of its properties in the U.S. and Canada take catering to older travelers very seriously and offer their Senior Saver Discounts to anyone over the age of 50. This means you will get 15 to 30 percent taken off the regular room rate when you make an advance reservation using the toll-free number. Because only a limited number of rooms

is set aside for this program, it pays to plan ahead. Without a reservation, your discount is 10 percent any day of
the year.
For information: Call your travel agent or 800-4 CHOICE
(800-424-6423).

CLARION INNS, HOTELS & RESORTS
See Choice Hotels. Call 800-CLARION (800-252-7466).

CLUB HOTELS BY DOUBLETREE
See Doubletree Hotels & Guest Suites. Call 800-222-8733.

CLUBHOUSE INNS & SUITES
This company, which runs a small group of inns mainly in
the Midwest, gives a 10 percent discount on the regular
room rates to guests over the age of 62. A unique extra benefit: when you stay one night before or after a major holiday such as Thanksgiving or Labor Day, the holiday night
is free. Advance reservations are required. A full breakfast
buffet and evening beverages are included.
For information: Call 800-258-2466.

COLONY HOTELS & RESORTS
Virtually all of Colony's hotels and condominium hotels in
the United States and Canada and its resorts in St. Thomas
give a 25 percent discount every day of the year to AARP
members. Nonmembers who are over 60 get a discount of
20 percent. Advance reservations are a must.
For information: Call 800-777-1700.

COMFORT INNS & SUITES
See Choice Hotels. Call 800-228-5150.

CONRAD INTERNATIONAL HOTELS

A subsidiary of Hilton Hotels, many Conrad Hotels in Europe, Australia, Hong Kong, Egypt, Singapore, Turkey, Uruguay, and the Caribbean participate in Hilton's Senior HHonors Worldwide program for over-60s. Members are entitled to up to 50 percent off the regular room rates and 20 percent off the bill for dinner for two. See Hilton Hotels.
For information: Call 800-432-3600.

COUNTRY HEARTH INNS

These economy motels in the South take up to 10 percent off the room rates for visitors over 50.
For information: Call 800-848-5767.

COUNTRY INNS & SUITES BY CARLSON

Each of these independently owned midprice inns all over the world gives you a minimum of 10 percent off the regular rates and a complimentary continental breakfast if you are at least 55 years old.
For information: Call 800-456-4000.

COURTYARD BY MARRIOTT

Here AARP or CARP members get 10 percent off the regular room rates every day of the year. There are about 400 of these moderately priced hotels, most of which feature swimming pools and exercise facilities. Advance reservations are recommended.
For information: Call 800-346-4000.

CROSS COUNTRY INNS

If you check in at one of these inns located in Ohio, Kentucky, and Michigan, you will get a discount of up to 25 percent on the regular room rates every day of the year; but you must belong to AARP, have a Golden Buckeye card, or have reached the age of 60.

For information: Call 800-621-1429.

CROWNE PLAZA HOTELS & RESORTS

At participating locations, if you belong to AARP or a few other senior organizations you are entitled to a minimum of 10 percent off the regular room rates most of the year, including holiday periods and weekends except for some special-event blackout days.

For information: Call 800-227-6963.

DAYS INNS

Join the September Days Club, the lodging industry's first senior travel club. If you are over 50 you'll be entitled to 15 to 50 percent discounts off the standard room rates at all 1,800 Days Inns worldwide. You'll also get 10 percent off at participating restaurants and gift shops whether you are a hotel guest or just stopping by. In addition, you are eligible for special rates on car rentals, airfares, cruises, theme parks, and sight-seeing attractions. A quarterly magazine keeps you up to date. Annual membership costs $15 and covers you and your spouse.

If you aren't a member of the club, you'll still get a 10 percent discount on your room rate anywhere in the world every day of the year if you show a membership card from AARP or CARP.

For information: Call 800-DAYS-INN (800-329-7466). In Canada, call 800-964-3434. To enroll in the September Days Club, call 800-241-5050.

DOUBLETREE HOTELS & GUEST SUITES

At all Doubletrees, members of AARP are given a 10 percent discount off the regular room rates—any time, any day, no advance reservations required. Members also get 10 percent off food and nonalcoholic beverages at participating Doubletree restaurants if they are hotel guests.
For information: Call 800-222-8733.

DOWNTOWNER MOTOR INNS

See Red Carpet Inn. Call 800-251-1962.

DRURY INNS

These economy motels concentrated in the Midwest offer a 5 to 10 percent discount on the regular room rates at all of their over 100 locations to anyone 50 or over. Just ask and have your proof of age handy.
For information: Call 800-325-8300.

ECONO LODGE

See Choice Hotels. Some rooms have been specially designed for mature travelers. Call 800-55 ECONO (800-553-2666).

ECONOMY INNS OF AMERICA

This economy lodging chain, with 20 motels located near major highways in California and Florida, gives 10 percent off the room rates to members of AARP. Just ask for it.
For information: Call 800-826-0778.

EMBASSY SUITES

In some of its 140 upscale all-suite hotels, Embassy Suites

gives a discount, usually about 10 percent, to travelers over the age of 55. That means you'll have to make inquiries when you make your reservations. Amenities for guests include a complimentary cooked-to-order breakfast every morning and free beverages every evening.

For information: Call 800-EMBASSY (800-362-2779).

FAIRFIELD INN

At Marriott's economy lodging chain, you will get 10 percent deducted from your bill, complimentary continental breakfast, and free local calls if you belong to AARP or CARP.

For information: Call 800-322-4000.

FOUR POINTS HOTELS

See Sheraton Hotels & Resorts. Call 800-325-3535.

HAMPTON INN & SUITES

The Lifestyle 50 Plus program at these 850 moderately priced hotels in the U.S., Canada, and Mexico allows up to four people to share the same room at a single room rate. Other benefits include rebates on hotel, air, car, and cruise travel booked through the member travel service; $20 in gas coupons; airline and car-rental coupons; 20 percent discount at over 4,000 restaurants nationwide; and more. A three-month trial membership costs $1; then unless you cancel you are automatically enrolled in the program for $59.95 a year.

For information: Call 800-HAMPTON (800-426-7866). For the Lifestyle 50 Plus program, call 800-204-4033.

HARLEY HOTELS

Look for a 10 percent discount at 14 Harley properties in the Northeast simply by flashing your AARP or other senior organization card. On weekends, however, the weekend rate may be a better bet.

For information: Call 800-321-2323.

HAWAIIAN HOTELS & RESORTS

At age 55, you'll be eligible for a 30 to 50 percent discount on the regular rates at any of these four hotels which are located on three Hawaiian islands, and sometimes other amenities are offered, such as free breakfast and a discount on car rentals. At two of the hotels, special senior packages that feature even better deals are also offered.

For information: Call 800-222-5642.

HAWTHORN SUITES HOTELS

AARP members and other guests over 65 get discounts of 30 to 45 percent at this group of suites hotels, most of them located in the southern states.

For information: Call 800-527-1133.

HILTON HOTELS

Hilton's Senior HHonors travel program is a very good deal for those over the age of 60 who do a lot of traveling. It gives you up to 50 percent off the regular rates at more than 400 Hilton and Conrad International Hotels around the world. Annual membership for you and your spouse is $55; a lifetime membership currently costs $290.

As a member, you may reserve a second room at the same reduced rate for family or friends who are traveling with you and get late checkout privileges when possible. You get 20 percent off the bill for dinner for two at participating hotel restaurants, whether or not you are guests of the hotel. You may also use the health facilities, where available, without charge.

Members are automatically enrolled in Hilton HHonors Worldwide, a guest reward program at Hiltons all over the world. It gives members both hotel points and airline frequent-flyer miles for each qualifying stay.

For those who don't join the Senior HHonors program but do belong to AARP, most Hiltons give a discount of 10 to 15 percent.

For information: Call 800-HILTONS (800-445-8667). To enroll in the Hilton Senior HHonors Worldwide, call 800-466-6677.

HISTORIC HOTELS OF AMERICA

All of these famous landmark hotels are individually owned and make their own decisions about offers to older guests. Here are some samples. The American Club in Kohler, Wisconsin, takes 15 percent off the regular rates for guests over 62. The Hotel Jerome in Aspen, Colorado, offers a 10 percent discount to AARP members, while the Hotel St. Francis in Santa Fe, New Mexico, does the same for visitors over 65. The Eagle Mountain House in Jackson, New Hampshire, offers those over 60 a 20 percent discount on midweek rates and 50 percent off the brunch buffet on Sundays. Both the Landmark Inn in Marquette, Michigan, and the Hotel San Carlos in Phoenix, Arizona, give a 10 percent discount to AARP members.

For information: Call the hotel directly. Or contact National

Trust Historic Hotels of America, 1785 Massachusetts Ave., NW, Washington, DC 20036; 202-588-6000.

HOLIDAY INN

Holiday Inn, with more than 3,100 hotels worldwide, intends to make major changes in its plans for older travelers. At this writing, however, those changes have not been completed. Meanwhile, its Holiday Inn Alumni travel club continues to be a good deal for travelers over the age of 50. It gives members a minimum of 20 percent off the regular room rates at its participating properties, including a continental breakfast for two.

Members also get 10 percent deducted from food bills in participating hotel restaurants in the U.S. and Canada anytime whether you're a guest at the hotel or just dropping by for a meal. On your birthday, you'll get a complimentary dinner when another meal is purchased, again whether you're staying at the hotel or not. And, during the Thanksgiving and Christmas holidays, the club rates and benefits are extended to members of your family, too, but you must make the reservations yourself directly with the hotel you choose.

To join Holiday Inn Alumni, call the toll-free number below or sign up at a participating hotel. The first year is free. After that, the membership costs $10 a year, a fee that is waived if you stay a minimum of five nights a year at any Holiday Inn.

All is not lost, however, if you don't join the club because AARP and CARP members get a minimum of 10 percent off regular rates at participating hotels.

For information: Call 800-HOLIDAY (800-465-4329) for

reservations. To enroll in the club, call 800-ALUMNI-2 (800-258-6642).

HOWARD JOHNSON HOTELS & INNS

At all of Howard Johnson's 550 locations in the U.S., Canada, Mexico, and other countries, members of AARP and CARP receive a discount of 20 percent off the regular rates on available rooms every day of the year. Just flash your membership card. All others over the age of 60 can get a 15 percent discount.

For information: Call 800-446-4656.

HYATT HOTELS & RESORTS

A collection of upscale hotels in the U.S., Canada, and the Caribbean, Hyatt always gives a discount of 15 to 25 percent off the regular room rates to guests over the age of 62. You must simply ask for it. Many Hyatts, mostly Hyatt Regencies, offer an even better deal: in cities and airports all over the country, seniors (again over 62) can get a special rate of $99 a night when rooms are available.

For information: Call 800-233-1234.

KIMPTON GROUP HOTELS

All of Kimpton's 21 hotels in cities on the West Coast, most of them in San Francisco, plus Denver and Chicago, have something good to offer mature travelers. The senior packages at these small, "boutique" hotels, each one different, give you discounts ranging from only a few dollars to more than a third off the regular room rates and often include breakfast, afternoon tea, and evening wine service. You must be a member of AARP or at least 55 in most cases to qualify as a senior.

For information: Call 800-546-2622 and ask for the telephone numbers of the individual hotels.

KNIGHTS INNS

This budget motel chain with more than 200 locations mostly in the East gives a discount of 10 percent every day of the year to anyone over 50.

For information: Call 800-843-5644.

LA QUINTA INNS

With over 300 locations in the U.S., these motor inns are inexpensive and become even more so when you ask for your 10 percent discount. You'll get it, except during special events, if you are a member of AARP or a similar organization or if you are 55 and can prove it.

For information: Call 800-531-5900.

LK INNS & LODGEKEEPER INNS

A budget chain in the Midwest, LK takes 10 percent off for AARP members and anybody else over 55.

For information: Call 800-282-5711.

THE LUXURY COLLECTION

See Sheraton Hotels & Resorts. Call 800-325-3535.

MAINSTAY SUITES

See Choice Hotels. Perks include continental breakfast. Call 800-660-MAIN (800-660-6246).

MARC RESORTS

If you are at least 55, a 25 percent discount is yours, subject to availability, at Marc Resorts' 20 locations on five Hawaiian islands.

For information: Call 800-535-0085.

MARRIOTT HOTELS, RESORTS & SUITES

Marriott's program for over-50s is among the best deals around if you are a member of AARP or CARP and can plan ahead. With a 21-day nonrefundable advance booking, you will get at least 50 percent off the regular rates at more than 200 participating locations worldwide. You must pay in advance for the entire stay by check or credit card when you make your reservation.

For those who can't commit themselves three weeks in the future, there is a flat 10 percent discount on regular room rates every day of the year for AARP or CARP card carriers.

In addition, you are offered a 20 percent discount on food and nonalcoholic beverages for your party of up to eight people. This may be used as often as you like, and you are not required to be an overnight guest to get this discount, but you must belong to AARP or CARP. Always ask first if the hotel or resort is participating in the discount plan.

And more: you'll get a 10 percent discount at participating gift shops.

Two hitches: the room discounts may not be available at all times, especially during peak periods, and some Marriotts do not participate in the seniors program.

For information: Call 800-228-9290.

MASTER HOSTS INNS & RESORTS

See Red Carpet Inn. Call 800-251-1962.

MOTEL 6

You can take advantage of a 10 percent discount on the room rates at these economy motels in more than 770 locations in the U.S. by showing your AARP or CARP card.
For information: Call 800-466-8356.

MOVENPICK HOTELS

News for travelers over 65: You pay only 65 percent of the room rate any day of the week at the Movenpick Hotels in Brussels, The Hague, and Hertogenbosch. Also, on selected days you pay only 65 percent of the menu price in the hotel restaurants. Rooms reserved for seniors are limited, so reserve yours early.
For information: Call 800-344-6835.

NATIONAL 9 INNS

You'll get a 10 percent discount at age 50 at most of these motels/hotels concentrated in the West.
For information: Call 800-524-9999.

NOVOTEL HOTELS

Eight of Novotel's nine hotels in the United States and Canada offer guests over the age of 55 their Golden Years rates that, subject to availability, can save them up to 50 percent off the published rates. At the Novotel Ottawa, however, you don't get the special rates unless you are 65.
For information: Call 800-668-6835.

OMNI HOTELS

Almost all of these upscale hotels—over 40 of them—take 10 percent off the published room rates every day of the week for members of AARP. Cardholders also get a 15 percent discount on food and nonalcoholic beverages in participating restaurants. To get the special room rate, reserve ahead and request the discount. In the restaurants, present your AARP card before you place your order.

For information: Call 800-THE-OMNI (800-843-6664).

ORION APARTMENT HOTELS

When you select one of Orion's studios or apartments in London, Paris, Brussels, Lisbon, or other European cities, all with fully equipped kitchenettes, you'll get a 10 percent discount off published rates any day of the year if you belong to AARP. You must make advance reservations.

For information: Call 800-987-6650.

OUTRIGGER HOTELS & RESORTS

If you are 50 or older, Outrigger's Fifty-Plus Program will give you 20 percent off regular published rates at its hotels and condos throughout Hawaii. You'll have your choice of a suite, an economy kitchenette, or a fully furnished condominium. Not only that, but you also will have the option of a rental car at $25 a day.

For members of AARP or CARP, the room discount is even better—25 percent all year on every room or suite except on packages or group rates.

For information: Call 800-OUTRIGGER (800-688-7444).

PARK INN & PARK PLAZA INTERNATIONAL

This group of hotels worldwide gives a 15 percent discount to members of AARP and guests over 60.

For information: Call 800-437-PARK (800-437-7275).

PASSPORT INN

See Red Carpet Inn. Call 800-251-1962.

QUALITY HOTELS & SUITES

See Choice Hotels. At suite hotels, you'll get a free cooked-to-order breakfast. Call 800-228-5151.

RADISSON HOTELS WORLDWIDE

At Radisson's more than 350 locations in 50 countries, take advantage of Senior Breaks, a discount of 25 to 40 percent off the standard rates. The age at which you qualify varies by country—in the U.S. and Canada, it's 50. In Europe, it is usually 65. You'll get the discount year-round, seven days a week, based on space availability. There's no club to join—just carry proof of your age. In addition, most Radissons offer you and your party a 15 percent discount on dining in hotel restaurants whether or not you are staying at the hotel, except in peak dining hours.

For information: Call 800-333-3333.

RAMADA LIMITEDS, INNS, AND PLAZA HOTELS

Ramada's Best Years Club, open to anyone at age 60, gives you 25 percent discounts, plus 15 frequent-stayer points for every dollar spent during your stays at hundreds of participating Ramadas. You'll get 3,000 bonus points when you sign up for the club and your accumulated points may be redeemed for free airline tickets, lodging, and travel awards. Other benefits include discounts on travel and car rentals and a quarterly newsletter. Lifetime membership costs $15. To join, sign up at any hotel or call the number below.

Another choice at participating Ramadas when space is available is a 15 percent discount for the over-50 members of AARP or CARP.

For information: Call 800-228-2828. To enroll in the Best Years Club, call 800-766-2378.

RAMADA HOTELS INTERNATIONAL

At these midscale hotels and resorts, most of them in Europe, if you are 60 years old or belong to AARP or another senior organization, you're entitled to the senior rate, a minimum of 25 percent off the regular room rates every day of the year. Ask for it when you make your reservations.

For information: Call 800-854-7854.

RED CARPET INN

Over 240 participating Hospitality International properties—which include Red Carpet Inn/Passport Inn/Downtowner Motor Inns, Master Host Inns, and Scottish Inn, located in the U.S., Jamaica, and the Bahamas—give 10 percent off the regular rates every day, all year, to members of AARP (subject, of course, to availability). Some inns also offer a discount, upwards of 5 percent, to nonmembers over the age of 65.

For information: Call 800-251-1962.

RED ROOF INNS

All you need to do is prove you are over 60 to get a 10 percent discount on the regular rates at this economy-lodging chain's more than 280 properties in 36 states.

For information: Call 800-843-7663.

RESIDENCE INN BY MARRIOTT

These extended-stay all-suite accommodations complete with kitchens offer members of AARP or CARP a 15 percent discount on regular rates every day of the year when space is available at participating locations. Complimentary continental breakfast, weekday social hours, and weekly barbecues are included.

For information: Call 800-331-3131.

RODEWAY INNS

See Choice Hotels. And check out Rodeway's new "senior-friendly" rooms, which feature such amenities as bright lighting, large clocks, grab bars, and big TV control buttons. Call 800-228-2000.

SANDMAN HOTELS

All situated in British Columbia and Alberta, these inns take 20 percent off the regular room rate if you are 55 or over. Show proof of age at check-in or, better yet, call the number below and ask for a 55 Plus Card. It's free.

For information: Call 800-726-3626.

SCOTTISH INN

See Red Carpet Inn. Call 800-251-1962.

DISNEY DISCOUNTS

If you are over the age of 55 and a fan of the famous Disney theme parks, inquire about a Magic Kingdom Club Gold Card. This is especially valuable if you plan at least a few visits per year. For a $50 two-year membership ($15 less than the regular adult price), you can get reduced admissions to all Disney theme parks worldwide. You'll also get 10 to 20 percent discounts at many Disney restaurants and resort hotels, plus savings on car rentals, cruises, and merchandise. Members receive a club newsletter that details events at Walt Disney World and Disneyland and a subscription to the Disney magazine.

At Disneyland Resort in California, there's more: at age 60, you're entitled to a small discount on the regular one-day ticket, and a 20 percent discount on the regular room rates at the Disneyland Hotel or the Disneyland Pacific Hotel.

Also keep in mind the Disneyland Flex Passport, which gives you entry to the park as often as you'd like during a five-consecutive-day period for the price of a regular two-day passport. This must be purchased through a travel agent. **For information:** For Walt Disney World, call 800-56-DISNEY (800-563-4763). For Disneyland, call 714-781-4565.

SHERATON HOTELS & RESORTS

All Sheratons around the world give you a break if you are over 60 or a member of AARP, CARP, or a long list of other recognized senior organizations, and are traveling for pleasure, not business. That's 15 to 25 percent off the published room rates, subject to availability. You may also reserve another room for family members at the senior rate when you are traveling together. Sometimes, however, these hotels have special sales going on that are better than the senior rate, so always ask for the best available price at the hotel you plan to visit. Affiliated hotels—The Luxury Collection and Four Points Hotels—give seniors the same discount at all of their locations.

As for the seven resort hotels in Hawaii, these offer a discount of 25 percent on regular rates to AARP members and all others over 55.

For information: Call 800-325-3535.

SHONEY'S INNS

Economy lodgings, Shoney's approximately 70 locations scattered throughout the southeastern states take 15 percent off the room rates for members of AARP and CARP any time, any day of the week. If you are not a member but are at least 55 years old, you will get a 10 percent discount when rooms are available.

For information: Call 800-222-2222.

SLEEP INNS

See Choice Hotels. Continental breakfast is included. Call 800-SLEEP INN (800-753-3746).

SONESTA INTERNATIONAL HOTELS

This collection of upscale hotels in the U.S., Egypt, Chile, and the Caribbean gives members of AARP a 15 percent discount off the regular rates. You must make reservations in advance, of course.

For information: Call 800-SONESTA (800-766-3782).

GOOD DEALS IN RESTAURANTS

Many restaurants offer special deals to people in their prime, but in most cases you must seek them out yourself by reading the menu, asking at the restaurant, or watching the ads in the local newspapers. At some big chains, such as the International House of Pancakes, Kentucky Fried Chicken, Applebee's, and Wendy's, there's a recommended corporate policy of senior discounts or special senior menus that may or may not be followed at its franchised restaurants.

Sometimes a senior discount is available any time you decide to dine, but often it's good only during certain hours or as "early bird" specials before 5 or 6 P.M. The eligible age varies from 55 to 65, and occasionally a restaurant requires that you sign up for its free senior club that issues you a membership card.

In addition, a few hotel chains will give you a break on your meal checks when you eat in their restaurants. For example:

At participating **Hilton Hotels** restaurants in the U.S. and Canada, you're entitled to a 20 percent discount on dinners for two, hotel guests or not, if one of you is a member of Hilton's Senior HHonors Worldwide.

Holiday Inn restaurants give a discount of 10 percent off your check when you dine there, whether or not you are a guest at the inn, if you belong to the Holiday Inn Alumni, a travel club for over-50s. On your birthday, your dinner is free when another meal is purchased.

The restaurants in the participating **Marriott Hotels and Resorts** will take 20 percent off your bill, except on alcoholic beverages, for a party of up to eight people if you belong to AARP or CARP, whether or not you are guests of the hotel.

If you join the September Days Club, you'll get room dis-counts at **Days Inns** worldwide and also a minimum of 10 percent off meals at participating locations.

Doubletree Hotels take 10 percent off the bill for food and nonalcoholic beverages in participating restaurants for mem-bers of AARP who are guests at the hotel.

At most **Omni Hotels** you'll get 15 percent taken off the check for food and nonalcoholic beverages in the hotel restaurants by flashing your AARP card.

You'll get a reduction of 15 percent on your food bills for yourself and your party when you eat at participating **Radis-son Hotels Worldwide** restaurants, whether or not you are hotel guests. You qualify for the savings at age 50 in U.S. locations and usually at 65 in Europe.

SPRINGHILL SUITES BY MARRIOTT

Make a reservation at one of these all-suite, moderately priced hotels and you'll get a 5 percent discount on the re-gular room rate if you belong to AARP or CARP. Included in the package are a complimentary continental breakfast and free local phone calls.

For information: Call 800-287-9400.

SUPER 8 MOTELS

Almost all of these over 1,700 no-frills economy motels in the U.S. and Canada give a discount, usually of 10 percent, to members of AARP and other older travelers.

For information: Call 800-800-8000.

SUSSE CHALETS

At these motels and inns scattered around the Northeast, you will get a room for up to four people for the price of a single room. You must be 60 or older to qualify.
For information: Call 800-5-CHALET (800-524-2538).

SWISSÔTEL

The Senior Specials program from Swissôtels gives members of AARP a 30 percent discount every day of the year, subject to space availability, on the regular room rates at all of its hotels in North America. Anyone over the age of 60 gets the same privilege. Advance reservations are required.
For Information: Call 800-737-9577.

TRAVELODGES HOTELS

All Travelodges and Thriftlodges, more than 500 of them in the U.S., Canada, Mexico, and Puerto Rico, have a nice straightforward plan for older travelers. This is a simple unrestricted 15 percent discount off the room rates any time, any night, for members of AARP and CARP when advance reservations are made through the toll-free number. A 10 percent discount is offered to everyone over 50 without reservations when rooms are available.
For information: Call 800-578-7878.

VAGABOND INNS

Vagabond's Smart Senior Program is one of the better deals around. It gives you 30 percent off the standard rates at age 55 at all except one of these economy inns on the West Coast. This group of hotels also has its Vagabuck Program,

which gives you $5 in play money every time you check out. Use it the next time you stay at a Vagabond Inn.
For information: Call 800-522-1555.

VILLAGER LODGES

At most of these economy extended-stay motels, you can get a room with a kitchenette at a discount of 10 percent off the daily rate if you belong to AARP or are over the age of 60.
For information: Call 800-328-7829.

WELLESLEY INNS

This group of inns located on the East Coast, mostly in Florida, gives members of AARP a discount of 10 percent off the regular room rates. Sometimes, however, there are special offers, so ask about them. Complimentary continental breakfast is included.
For information: Call 800-444-8888.

WESTCOAST HOTELS

If you are over 55, ask for the senior rate at these midscale hotels in the western states and Hawaii. The rate varies by location.
For information: Call 800-426-0670.

WESTIN HOTELS & RESORTS

Many of these luxury hotels offer special rates and packages for seniors, but each has its own policy, so always ask about the possibilities when you make reservations. And if you are a member of United Silver Wings Plus, you will get your room at 50 percent off the published rate at participating hotels.

For information: Call 800-937-8461.

WINGATE INNS

A hotel chain with midscale prices for rooms with high-tech amenities, Wingate Inns gives a 10 percent discount off published room rates to members of a large number of senior organizations including AARP.

For information: Call 800-228-1000.

WYNDHAM HOTELS & RESORTS

Wyndham's offer to mature guests is very simple: members of AARP get 20 percent off corporate rates on weekdays (Sunday through Thursday) and 20 percent off the lowest weekend rates on Friday and Saturday nights, with a few blackout dates.

For information: Call 800-WYNDHAM (800-996-3426).

WYNDHAM GRAND HERITAGE HOTELS

At this group of upscale inns in the U.S., all restored *grande dame* hotels with historical significance, the Wyndham discounts described above are valid for members of AARP: 20 percent off corporate rates on weekdays and 20 percent off the lowest weekend rates on Fridays and Saturdays when rooms are available.

For information: Call 800-996-3426.

11

Alternative Lodgings for Thrifty Wanderers

I f you're willing to be innovative, imaginative, and occasionally fairly spartan, you can travel for a song or thereabouts. Here are some novel kinds of lodgings that can save you money and perhaps offer adventures in the bargain. Not all of them are designed specifically for people over 50, but each reports that the major portion of its clientele consists of free spirits of a certain age who like to travel, appreciate good values for their money, and enjoy meeting new people from other places.

For more ways to cut travel costs and get smart at the same time, check out the residential/educational programs in Chapter 16.

AFFORDABLE TRAVEL CLUB

Join this bed-and-breakfast club limited to people over 40 and you'll pay a pittance for accommodations, meet interesting people, and see new places. You may join as a host member, putting up other travelers in your spare bedroom a couple of times a year and providing breakfast and a little of your time to acquaint your guests with your area. Visitors pay $15 for a single or $20 for a double per night for their stay. In return, you get to stay in other people's homes for the same token fee when you travel. Or you may prefer to be a nonhost member, using the guest privileges only and paying $25 for a single or $30 for a double per night.

There are currently about 1,000 members in this club in 45 states and 21 countries offering accommodations ranging from simple bedrooms to suites and condos. The annual host membership fee per household is $50, while a nonhost membership costs $90 a year. It entitles you to a quarterly newsletter and a directory that lists and describes the host homes. The club also sponsors a group tour at least once a year.

If you have a pet, you may want to take advantage of the club's house-sitting and pet-sitting service—members move into your house and care for your house and/or pets while you're on vacation, meanwhile enjoying a visit to your neighborhood in exchange.

For information: Affordable Travel Club, 6556 Snug Harbor Ln., Gig Harbor, WA 98335; 253-858-2172.

AMERICAN-INTERNATIONAL HOMESTAYS

Travel to a foreign land and stay in the homes of local residents. Immerse yourself in the country's customs and traditions, with your English-speaking hosts acting as your personal guides and interpreters. You'll have your own bedroom in the hosts' home and become part of the family, eating meals and exploring your surroundings together. An inexpensive way to travel, homestays provide a unique way to experience other cultures. AIH handles all the travel arrangements for individuals or groups for stays all over the world, from Australia, Belgium, China, Ecuador, Germany, India, Latvia, and Lithuania to Mongolia, Ukraine, Uzbekistan, and the Kyrgyz Republic.

For information: American-International Homestays, PO Box 1754, Nederland, CO 80466; 800-876-2048 or 303-642-3088.

DEL WEBB'S SUN CITIES

Eight Sun Cities operated by the Del Webb Corporation offer Vacation Getaway programs designed to let you sample the lifestyle there just in case you're thinking of moving to one of these "active adult communities." For remarkably little, you'll have your own villa for three, four, or seven nights starting any day of the week and enjoy all the facilities: tennis, golf, swimming, aerobics, massages, and socializing with residents and staff. Depending on the season and the location, the rates range from about $179 for three nights all year to about $575 for a seven-day package in the high season.

The only requirements are that one partner in a visiting couple is at least 55 years old and no one in your party is under 19. You may stay no more than twice at the same location.

The communities currently offering Vacation Getaways include Sun City Grand in Phoenix, Sun City MacDonald Ranch and Sun City Summerlin in Las Vegas, Sun City

Palm Desert in Palm Springs, Sun City Roseville in Sacramento, Sun City Hilton Head, Sun City Georgetown in Austin, Texas, and Spruce Creek in Ocala, Florida.
For information: Sun Cities, 6001 N. 24th St., Phoenix, AZ 85016; 800-4-DEL WEBB (800-433-5932).

ELDERHOSTEL HOMESTAYS

Elderhostel collaborates with World Learning, a 65-year-old institution specializing in international education and homestays, to place hostelers in the homes of local families in many foreign countries. The Homestay Programs—two to three weeks long—begin with a week of lectures, classes, and field trips to introduce you to the local history and culture. Then you move into your host home to spend a few days as a member of the family. Those participating in three-week programs meet for an additional week of classes and excursions before heading home.
For information: Elderhostel, Dept. M2, PO Box 1959, Wakefield, MA 01880; 877-426-8056 (toll free) or 617-426-7788.

EVERGREEN BED & BREAKFAST CLUB

This bed-and-breakfast club exclusively for people over the age of 50 was founded in 1982 and now has about 4,000 members and 2,000 host homes in the United States and Canada as well as a few in Mexico and Europe. Whether a host home is elegant or simple, members pay only $10 a day single or $15 a day per couple to stay in the homes of other members. In return, they welcome members of the club into their own homes as often as they wish.

When you join, you receive an annual directory with relevant information about all of the host families and the special attractions of their areas. You then make your own arrangements for visits and pay the gratuities directly to the hosts. A quarterly newsletter provides the latest information. Annual club dues are $40 single and $50 per couple.

An important asset of this hospitality club is the opportunity for members to make new friends and perhaps travel together, as many members do. Group tours and cruises are now offered to the membership, with current ventures including a Volga River cruise in Russia, an Amazon River cruise in Brazil, and a luxury train trip in South Africa.
For information: Evergreen Bed and Breakfast Club, PO Box 1430, Falls Church, VA 22041; 800-962-2392.

THE MILITARY RETIREES' BED & BREAKFAST CLUB

This new travel club, open only to retirees from any of the U.S. armed forces and NOAA and their families, provides a wide selection of low-cost lodgings through its membership network. Members, who pay annual dues of $39.50 (and a one-time registration fee of $10), agree to host an occasional fellow retiree overnight, provide a continental breakfast, and give information about points of interest in their communities and the immediate area. In return, they may stay with other hosts when they travel. Cost of lodging is $29.50 for two adults or $25 for a single, including breakfast. Free one-year memberships are offered to most members of organizations such as TROAA, American Legion, and VFW, all of which support the welfare of military retirees.

For information: The Military Retirees' Bed and Breakfast Club, PO Box 1751, Maple Grove, MN 55311; 800-273-0511.

NEW PALTZ SUMMER LIVING

Think about spending a couple of the hottest months in the mountains, about 75 miles north of New York City. Every summer, while the usual student occupants are on vacation, 140 furnished garden apartments are reserved for seniors in the village of New Paltz, near Mohonk Mountain and home of a branch of the State University of New York. The rents at this writing for the entire summer (from early June until late August) range from $1,325 to $3,600, depending on the size of the apartment. Living right in town next to the campus, you may audit college courses free, attend lectures and cultural events, and take part in planned activities in the clubhouse. There is a heated pool and a tennis court in the complex. Buses travel to New York frequently for those who want to go to the theater, and there are frequent day trips to places of interest.

For information: New Paltz Summer Living, 19 E. Colonial Dr., New Paltz, NY 12561; 800-431-4143 or 914-255-7205.

RETREAT CENTER GUEST HOUSES

If you are seeking a refuge from the pressures of daily life and time for quiet reflection, a stay at a retreat center may be your answer. Retreat centers are church-affiliated compounds where guests of any religious preference (or none at all) and of any age may find lodging and three meals for $35 to $45 a day. *Retreat Center Guest House Guide*, available from CTS Publications, describes more than 850 such centers in the U.S., Canada, Europe, New Zealand, and Australia.

For information: CTS Publications, PO Box 8355, Newport Beach, CA 92660; 949-720-3729.

ROBSON COMMUNITIES

The Preferred Guest Program invites prospective adult home-buyers to stay a few days at one of the three Robson Communities in Arizona—one near Chandler, another outside of Phoenix, and the third north of Tucson. Here they may sample the "active adult resort lifestyle" complete with clubhouses, swimming pools, tennis courts, spas, and golf courses. As a guest, you'll stay on-site in a furnished two-bedroom home, play a round of golf, have a dinner with residents, use the recreational facilities, and spend a few hours with a salesperson. Depending on the time of year, prices currently range from $99 (in summer) to $299 (in winter) for a three-night stay. One person in your party must be at least 40 and no one under 19 may participate.

For information: Robson Communities, 9532 E. Riggs Rd., Sun Lakes, AZ 85248; 800-732-9949.

ROYAL COURT APARTMENTS

As an alternative to hotels, one-, two-, and three-bedroom apartments are available all year at the Royal Court in central London, one block from Hyde Park, giving you plenty of space and a home at the end of a busy day. You'll get a discount of 10 percent if you are over 50 and mention this book when you make your reservations.

For information: Royal Court Apartments, British Network Ltd., 594 Valley Rd., Upper Montclair, NJ 07043; 800-274-8583 or 201-744-5215.

SENIORS ABROAD

The Seniors Abroad homestay program pairs American travelers with host families for visits of three to four weeks in Japan or Australia/New Zealand. Participtants live as family members in three to five different homes during their stay in the host country, learning firsthand about local cultures and lifestyles. Hosts act as tour guides, introducing visitors to their communities and the nearby sights.

American families, in turn, invite guests from the same countries to their own homes, and Seniors Abroad is always seeking new volunteers for this part of the program. All hospitality is voluntary on the part of the hosts and without cost to the guests, except for travel, tours, and brief hotel stays.

For information: Seniors Abroad, 12533 Pacato Circle North, San Diego, CA 92128; 619-485-1696.

SERVAS

The oldest of the hospitality clubs, Servas is an international cooperative system of hosts and travelers established to help promote world peace, goodwill, and understanding among peoples. A nonprofit, nongovernmental, interracial, and interfaith organization open to all ages, it provides approved travelers with a list of hosts—over 14,000 in all—in 138 countries, including the U.S., who welcome members to stay in their homes free of charge. To participate, you make your own arrangements to visit hosts, usually for two days at a time. The hospitable people, all peace activists, who offer to share their space with you are eager to learn about you and your culture. You may do the same for other travelers in return, if you wish.

Travelers must pay a yearly membership fee of $65 (U.S.) or $50 (Canada), good for unlimited travel, and are asked for two letters of reference and an interview. Hosts in the U.S. are asked for a voluntary donation of at least $35 per year.

For information: Send a #10 self-addressed, stamped envelope to US Servas, 11 John St., Room 407, New York, NY 10038; 212-267-0252. In Canada: Servas Canada, 229 Hillcrest Ave., Toronto, ON M2N 3P3.

SUN CITY CENTER

Located about 25 miles outside of Tampa, Florida, Sun City Center wants you to see what a 5,000-acre, self-contained retirement community is all about. It offers an inexpensive vacation package so you can sample the lifestyle there. You may stay for a few days, lodging at a motel on the grounds, and take part in all of the activities. A stay of four days, three nights with daily continental breakfast, tennis, swimming, and access to club facilities currently costs $99 to $189, depending on the season. One member of your party must be 55 or older and an extensive tour of the town with a salesperson is on the agenda.

For information: Sun City Center, PO Box 5698, Sun City Center, FL 33571; 800-237-8200.

12

Perks in Parks and Other Good News

Here and there throughout the United States and Canada, enterprising officials in states, provinces, and cities have initiated some enticing programs designed to capture the imagination of the mature population. Often they are expressing their appreciation of our many contributions to society and simply want to do something nice for us. And sometimes they are trying to attract us and our vacation dollars to their vicinity, having discovered that we're always eager to enjoy ourselves and know a good deal when we see one.

But, first, keep in mind:

■ Before you set off for a new place, it's a good idea to write ahead for free maps, calendars of events, booklets describing sites and scenes of interest, accommodation guides, and perhaps even a list of special discounts or other good things that are available to you as a person over 50.

■ Many states offer passes to their state parks and recreation facilities free or at reduced prices to people who are old enough to have learned how to treat those areas respectfully.

■ After the section on national parks, you'll find information about state park passes and special events in many states. There may be other good deals that have escaped our attention, but those in this chapter are probably the cream of the crop.

ESCAPEES CLUB

Escapees is a club dedicated to providing a support network for RVers, full-time or part-time, most of whom are on the far side of 50. It publishes a bimonthly magazine filled with useful information for travelers who carry their homes with them, organizes rallies in the U.S., Canada, and Mexico, and hosts five-day seminars on RV living. Other benefits include discounted co-op RV parks and campgrounds, emergency road service, mail service, and voice message service. After a $10 fee to join, the annual membership fee is $50 a year.

The club has established its own CARE Center (Continuing Assistance for Retired Escapees), a separate RV campground where retired members can live independently in their own RVs while receiving medical and living assistance, housekeeping, and transportation services as needed.

For information: Escapees Inc., 100 Rainbow Drive, Livingston, TX 77351; 888-757-2582 or 409-327-8873.

NATIONAL PARKS

GOLDEN AGE PASSPORT

Available for $10 to anyone over 62, this lifetime pass admits you free of charge to all of the federal government's parks, forests, refuges, monuments, and recreation areas that charge entrance fees. Anybody who accompanies you in the same car or RV also gets in free. If you turn up at the gate in a commercial vehicle such as a van or bus, the passport admits you and your spouse, your children, and even your parents, so remember to take them along.

You will also get a 50 percent discount on federal use fees charged for facilities and services such as camping, boat launching, parking, or cave tours.

The passport is not available by mail. You must pick one up in person at any National Park System area where entrance fees are charged or at any offices of the National Park Service, the U.S. Forest Service, the Fish and Wildlife Service, or the Bureau of Land Management. You must have proof of age. A driver's license will do just fine.

(The free Golden Access Passport provides the same benefits for the disabled of any age. The Golden Eagle Passport, for those under 62, costs $25 per year.)

For information: National Park Service, PO Box 37127, Washington, DC 20013.

CANADIAN NATIONAL PARKS

The national parks and national historic sites throughout Canada charge modest entry fees for adults and take 25 percent off those for seniors. The same is generally true for provincial parks.

OFFERINGS FROM THE STATES

Virtually every state has a special senior rate for hunting and fishing licenses for people over a certain age (usually 65). Some states require no license at all for seniors, while others give you a reduced fee (usually half). Most require that you are a resident of the state to get these privileges. Most states also offer state park discounts to seniors, usually only residents, reducing or eliminating entrance fees and marking down camping rates. To check out the regulations in your state or a state you are visiting, call the state or local parks department or the state tourism office.

For a free listing of all the state tourism offices and their toll-free numbers, send a self-addressed, stamped envelope to Discover America, Travel Industry Association of America, 1100 New York Ave. NW, Ste. 450, Washington, DC 20005.

CALIFORNIA

Campers 62 or over get $2 taken off admissions and overnight camping fees in all state parks. Just show your ID at the gate.

For information: For campsite reservations call 800-444-7275 .

If you are going to visit Long Beach, call ahead for the *Senior Saver Getaway Guide.* It lists the senior discounts at some of this city's hotels and attractions.

For information: Long Beach Area Convention and Visitors Bureau, 1 World Trade Center, Long Beach, CA 90831; 800-452-7829.

Carmel on the Monterey Peninsula also has some literature for you. It offers *Carmel's Escape for Seniors*, a free brochure describing a few discounts for people over the age of 55 at galleries, theaters, restaurants, shops, and accommodations. The catch: the discounts are not valid on Fridays or Saturdays or any time during July or August.

For information: Carmel Business Assn., PO Box 4444, Carmel, CA 93921; 800-550-4333 or 408-624-2522.

COLORADO

The Aspen Leaf Pass entitles Colorado residents 62 and over to free entrance to state parks any day and camping Sundays through Thursdays. The pass costs $10 per year.

For information: Colorado Division of State Parks, 1313 Sherman St., Room 618, Denver CO 80203; 303-866-3437.

CONNECTICUT

Residents of Connecticut who are over 65 get a free lifetime Charter Oak Pass that gets them into state parks and forests plus Gillette Castle, Dinosaur Park, and Quinebaug Valley Hatchery for free. To get your pass, write to the address below and send along a copy of your current Connecticut driver's license.

For information: DEP, Charter Oak Pass, State Parks Division, DEP, 79 Elm St., Hartford, CT 06106; 860-424-3200.

FLORIDA

Orlando, one of the most popular destinations in the U.S. today, is visited by an estimated 3.3 million "mature visitors" a year. To accommodate these travelers, the city distributes a free *Mature Traveler Discount Brochure* that lists significant senior savings, most of them valid for anyone over the age of 50 or 55, at hotels, tourist attractions, water parks, dinner shows, museums, and more. The city also offers a free Orlando Magicard for all ages, which offers even more discounts.

For information: Pick up the brochures at the Official Visitor Center, 8723 International Dr., Ste. 101, Orlando, FL 32821; or get them by mail by calling 800-551-0181 or 407-363-5872.

Visit Marathon in the Florida Keys in the month of November and you will get special savings when some hotels, diving facilities, fishing charters, and restaurants offer seniors 15 to 50 percent off their rates. There are special events planned for you during the month as well. Send for the free Senior Discount Card and a brochure describing other offers and discounts in the Keys.

For information: Call 800-262-7284 or 305-743-5417.

INDIANA

The Golden Hoosier Passport admits Indiana residents over the age of 60 and fellow passengers in a private vehicle to all state parks and natural resources without charge. An application for the passport, which costs $5 a year, is available at all state parks or from the Indiana State Parks Department.

For information: Indiana State Parks Dept., 402 W. Washington St., Room W298, Indianapolis, IN 46204; 317-232-4124.

MAINE

Pick up your free Senior Citizen Pass and you will pay no day-use fees at Maine state parks and historic sites. The pass is available at any state park or by writing to the Bureau of Parks and Lands and including proof of your age.

For information: Maine Bureau of Parks and Lands, State House Station 22, Augusta, ME 04333; 207-287-3821.

MICHIGAN

You can get some good deals in Michigan if you are a resident who's reached the age of 65. These include a motor-vehicle permit that gets you into all state parks for $5 a year, a fishing license with an annual fee of $1 a year, and a hunting license that costs $4 a year.

For information: Call the Department of Natural Resources at 517-373-9900.

MISSOURI

Missouri residents over the age of 60 are entitled to a free Silver Citizen Discount Card that gives them discounts at restaurants, stores, services, pharmacies, and other businesses throughout the state. To get a card, call the toll-free number below.

For information: Missouri Dept. of Social Services, PO Box 1337, Jefferson City, MO 65102; 800-235-5503.

MONTANA

You need pay only half the usual camping fee in Montana's state parks if you are over the age of 62.

For information: Montana Fish, Wildlife, and Parks Dept., 1420 E. 6th Ave., Helena, MT 59620; 406-444-4041.

NEVADA

In Carson City, you will strike silver without doing any digging—if you are over 50 and join the free Seniors Strike Silver Club. You'll get a list of discounts in town, plus a membership card to present as identification to participating merchants.

For information: Carson City Convention & Visitors Bureau, 1900 S. Carson St., Carson City, NV 89701; 800-NEVADA-1 (800-638-2321).

NEW MEXICO

For a brochure listing senior discounts at attractions, stores, hotels, restaurants, and transportation in Albuquerque, call the toll-free number below.

For information: Albuquerque Convention & Visitors Bureau; 800-733-9918, ext. 3340.

NEW YORK

Simply by presenting your current valid New York driver's license or a New York nondriver's identification card, you will be entitled to all of the privileges of the Golden Park Program for residents over the age of 62. The program offers, any weekday except holidays, free vehicle access to state parks and arboretums, free entrance to state historic sites, and reduced fees for state-operated swimming, golf, tennis, and boat rentals. Just show your driver's license or ID card to the guard at each facility as you enter.

For information: State Parks, Albany, NY 12238; 518-474-0456.

OHIO

When residents of Ohio turn 60 they receive a free Golden Buckeye Card, which entitles them to discounts, typically about 10 percent, on goods and services at thousands of participating businesses throughout the state. They are also given the opportunity to receive a free quarterly magazine for seniors.

For information and the sign-up site nearest your home: Golden Buckeye Unit, Ohio Dept. of Aging, 50 W. Broad St., 9th floor, Columbus, OH 43215; 800-422-1976 or 614-466-5500.

PENNSYLVANIA

Send for a free brochure called *Philadelphia Mature Travelers Discounts* for a list of discounts available in this historic city. It lists dozens of Philadelphia sites and attractions, restaurants, hotels, tours, museums, stores, and cultural events that offer special discounts for visitors over 50.

More good news for seniors in Philadelphia, whether visitors or residents, is the free transportation offered by SEPTA, the regional railway, bus, trolley, and subway system. If you are over 65 and have a Medicare, Railroad Retirement Annuity, or Senior Citizen Transit Identification card, you may ride free weekdays from 9 A.M. to 3:30 P.M., 6:30 P.M. to 6 A.M., and all day weekends and holidays. On the regional rail lines, you ride free or at reduced rates on all off-peak trains if you have the proper ID card.

For information: Philadelphia Visitors Center, 16th Street and JFK Blvd., Philadelphia, PA 19102; 800-537-7676. For information about SEPTA, call 215-580-7800.

SOUTH CAROLINA

Residents of South Carolina who are 65 or older must merely show their driver's licenses to get free admission at all state parks, plus half off on both the camping fees at all parks and the greens fees at Hickory Knob and Cheraw State Parks.

For information: South Carolina Department of Parks, Recreation, and Tourism, 1205 Pendleton St., Columbia, SC 29201; 803-734-0166.

TENNESSEE

Anyone over the age of 62, state resident or not, gets a 10 percent discount on food at park restaurants, cabins, and rooms at the Resort Park Inns. Tennessee residents over 62 are charged only 50 percent of the regular camping fees, while out-of-state campers are entitled to a 25 percent reduction. Admission to all state parks is free, regardless of your age.

For information: Tennessee State Parks, 401 Church St., LC Tower, Nashville, TN 37243; 800-421-6683.

UTAH

The Silver Card issued by Park City, an old mining town known for its great ski mountains, is a free summer program of discounts that gives you 10 percent or more off on merchandise, tickets, and meals. Pick up your card and an information packet for seniors at a participating hotel or the Park City Visitors Bureau.

For information: Park City Convention and Visitors Bureau, 1910 Prospector Ave., Park City, UT 84060; 800-453-1360 or 801-649-6100.

GOOD SAM CLUB

The **Good Sam Club** is an international organization of people who travel in recreational vehicles, mentioned here because the vast majority of those in rolling homes are over 50. Its goal is to make RVing safer, more enjoyable, and less expensive. Among the benefits are 10 percent discounts on nightly fees at over two thousand RV parks and campgrounds, plus more discounts on propane, parts, and accessories at hundreds of service centers.

The club offers a toll-free hotline, a lost-key service, lost-pet service, trip routing, mail forwarding, telephone message service, insurance, a magazine, and campground directories. Most important, it provides low-cost emergency road service anywhere in the U.S. and Canada, including Alaska. Social activities include Good Sam rallies and travel tours and cruises all over the world. And about 2,100 local chapters in the U.S. and Canada hold campouts and meetings and participate in local volunteer projects. Membership is $25 a year per family, $44 for two years, $59 for three.

For information: The Good Sam Club, PO Box 6885, Englewood, CO 80155; 800-234-3450.

VERMONT

Vermont's residents over 60 may purchase a Green Mountain Passport for $2 from their own town clerk. It is good for a lifetime and entitles them to free or reduced day-use admission at any Vermont State Park and its programs. Other benefits include discounts on concerts, restaurant meals, prescriptions, and more.

For information: Vermont Dept. of Aging, 103 S. Main St., Waterbury, VT 05676; 802-241-2400.

VIRGINIA

In this state that abounds with historical sites, you'll find senior discounts almost everywhere you go. You'll get them, for example, at Colonial Williamsburg, Busch Gardens, Berkeley Plantation, Mount Vernon, Woodlawn Plantation, Gunston Hall Plantation, the Edgar Allan Poe Museum in Richmond, and the Virginia Air and Space Center.

For information: Virginia Division of Tourism, 1021 E. Cary St., Richmond, VA 23219; 800-786-4484.

WASHINGTON, D.C.

The Golden Washingtonian Club is a discount program in the nation's capital for people over 55. With proof of age, both residents and visitors may get discounts from about 1,700 merchants listed in the *Gold Mine Directory*, free at many hotels or at the Washington Visitor Information Center. More than 30 hotels offer 10 to 40 percent off regular rates, many restaurants take a percentage off meals, and many retail stores do the same for purchases.

For information: Family and Child Services of Washington, D.C., 929 L St. NW, Washington, DC 20001; 202-289-1510, ext. 186.

WEST VIRGINIA

Everybody who turns 60 in West Virginia gets a Golden Mountaineer Discount Card, which entitles the bearer to discounts from more than 3,500 participating merchants and professionals in the state and a few outside of it. If you don't receive a card from the state soon after your 60th birthday, you may apply for one at your local senior center or by calling the number below. Flash it wherever you go and save a few dollars.

For information: West Virginia Bureau of Senior Services, 1900 Kanawha Blvd. East, Charleston, WV 25305; 304-558-3317.

13

Good Deals for Good Sports

Real sports never give up their sneakers. If you've been a physically active person all your life, you're certainly not going to become inert now—especially since you've probably got more time, energy, and maybe funds, than you ever had before to enjoy athletic activities. Besides, you can now take advantage of some interesting special privileges and adventures offered exclusively to people over 49.

The choices described here are not for those whose interest in sports is limited to watching football games on television or sitting on hard benches in stadiums with cans of beer. They are for energetic people who do the running themselves.

AMERICAN WILDERNESS EXPERIENCE

Action vacations are the specialty of AWE (see Chapter 3), an agency that offers trips from a great many tour operators. You may choose from a long list of adventures ranging from horseback trips to sailing, canoeing, kayaking, hiking, trekking, dog sledding, scuba diving, biking, cross-country skiing, and other vigorous options, some of them specifically for people over 50.

For information: American Wilderness Experience, Inc., PO Box 1486, Boulder, CO 80306; 800-444-0099 or 303-444-2622.

ELDERHOSTEL

Many Elderhostel programs (see Chapter 16) include an active sport or two among their courses. Look through the catalog and you'll find a wide selection of outdoor activities for beginners as well as experienced athletes. Among the choices are golf, walking, tennis, hiking, biking, sea kayaking, sailing, whitewater rafting, wilderness canoeing, skiing, snowshoeing, and trail biking.

For information: Elderhostel, 75 Federal St., Boston, MA 02110; 877-426-8056 (toll free) or 617-426-7788. In Canada: Elderhostel Canada, 5 Cataraqui St., Kingston, ON K7K 1Z7; 613-530-2222.

EXPLORATIONS IN TRAVEL

Specializing in outdoor and cultural vacations for women over 40, Explorations in Travel features action-filled itineraries geared for energetic women who love the outdoors and like to travel with contemporaries. Trips include inn-to-inn hiking and canoeing in Vermont, sailing in the Greek islands, walking in the French Pyrenees, cross-country skiing in Minnesota, and exploring along the Georgia coast. At least one multigenerational trip is planned each year, along with more conventional vacations just for women.

For information: Explorations in Travel, 1922 River Rd., Guilford, VT 05301; 802-257-0152.

THE OVER THE HILL GANG

This is a club that welcomes fun-loving, adventurous, people over 50 (and younger spouses) who are looking for action and contemporaries to pursue it with. No naps, no rockers, no sitting by the pool sipping planter's punch. The Over the Hill Gang started as a ski club many years ago but its members can now be found participating in all kinds of activities. Recent trips have included skiing at Keystone, Taos, Steamboat, Vail, Big Sky, and other ski areas in the West, Val d'Isere in France, Valle Nevado in Chile, and in New Zealand; plus whitewater rafting in Idaho, biking on Cape Cod and in Hawaii, rafting in the Grand Canyon, golfing in the Canadian Rockies.

The club currently has about 5,500 members in 50 states and 14 countries and 11 regional "gangs" (chapters). Each local gang decides on its own activities. If there's no chapter in your vicinity, you may become a member-at-large and participate in any of the activities.

The annual membership fee ($40 single, $65 for a couple) brings you a quarterly magazine, discounts, information about national and chapter events, and a chance to join the fun. The local gangs charge small additional yearly dues. *For information:* Over the Hill Gang International, 1820 W. Colorado Ave., Colorado Springs, CO 80904; 719-389-0022.

ADVENTURES FOR BIKERS

Biking has become one of America's most popular sports, and people who never dreamed they could go much farther than around the block are now pedaling up to 50 miles in a day. That includes over-the-hill bikers as well as youngsters of 16, 39, or 49. In fact, some tours and clubs are designated specifically for over-50s.

COMPASS HOLIDAYS

For a "cycling break" in the heart of England—the Cotswolds, Thames Valley, Oxford, Stratford, Cirencester— look into the guided or self-planned biking tours from Compass Holidays. With a guide you can ride for three days, for example, around Bourton-on-the-Water, or seven days in the Cotswolds, starting and ending in Cheltenham. You can also ride on your own with maps and planned accommodations on circular routes along quiet country roads from village to village near Bath or Malmesbury. Your luggage is transported for you. For bikers over 50, this tour company—which also schedules walking tours—offers a 10 percent discount if you take a tour of at least two nights and mention this book. Take your own bike or rent one there.

For information: Compass Holidays, 48 Shurdington Rd., Cheltenham, Gloucestershire GL53 OJE, UK; +44 (0) 1242-250642; E-mail: compass.holidays@dial.pipex.com.

THE CROSS CANADA CYCLE TOUR SOCIETY

This is a bicycling club for retired people who love to jump on their bikes and take off across the countryside. Most of the club's members are over 60, with many in their 70s and 80s and only a few under 50. Says the society, "Our aim is to stay alive as long as possible." Now there's a worthwhile goal.

Based in Vancouver, B.C., with members—both men and women, skilled and novice—mostly in B.C., Ontario, and Alberta, it organizes many trips a year, all led by volunteer tour guides. Membership costs $25 single or $35 per couple and includes a monthly newsletter to keep you up to date on happenings. Several times a week, local members gather for day rides, and several times a year there are longer club trips to such far-ranging locations as the San Juan Islands, Waterton Park in Canada and Glacier National Park in the U.S., Australia, Hawaii's Big Island, Arizona, New Zealand, and Denmark. Every few years a group of intrepid bikers pedals clear across Canada, an adventure that takes a few weeks to accomplish, with some members dropping in and out along the way. Many of the longer trips are tenting or camping tours, while others put you up in hostels, motels, or hotels.

For information: Cross Canada Cycle Tour Society, 6943 Antrim Ave., Burnaby, BC V5J 4M5; 604-433-7710.

ELDERHOSTEL BICYCLE TOURS

Elderhostel's famous educational travel programs include both domestic and foreign bicycle tours among its many offerings. These vary by the season and the year and are all listed in the organization's frequent and voluminous catalogs. Recent tours in the U.S. have included six-day inn-to-inn pedals along the Erie Canal in New York State, the northwest corner of Arizona, and the rolling hills of Texas. Lectures and sight-seeing are included.

Bike tours in foreign lands are scheduled weekly from

April through September in Bermuda, Denmark, England, Italy, Germany, Austria, France, and the Netherlands. Led by a guide and riding as a group, you cover 25 to 35 miles a day and learn about the culture and history from local educators and other specialists. Three-speed bikes are provided, as are breakfast and dinner and accommodations in small hotels. The support van that travels with the group to carry the luggage and repair equipment will carry you too if you decide you can't possibly make it up another hill. *For information:* Elderhostel, 75 Federal St., Boston, MA 02110; 877-426-8056 (toll free) or 617-426-7788. In Canada: Elderhostel Canada, 5 Cataraqui St., Kingston ON K7K 1Z7; 613-530-2222.

INTERNATIONAL BICYCLE TOURS

The Fifty Plus Tour run by IBT is planned for people over 50 who are not into pedaling up mountains but love to cycle. The trip goes to Holland in May and takes you on a leisurely trip along bicycle paths and quiet country roads on flat terrain through farmland and quaint villages. You'll cover only about 30 miles a day, so there is plenty of time for sight-seeing, snacking, shopping, and relaxing. You lodge in small hotels and dine on local specialties.

Although this is the only tour strictly limited to over-50s, many older bikers are found on IBT's other bike tours to Holland, Denmark, England, Ireland, Italy, France, Bermuda, Austria, Cape Cod, Charleston, the Chesapeake and Ohio Canal, Nantucket, and Florida. And, of course, many more sign on for Elderhostel's bike tours (in Bermuda, England, France, the Netherlands, Austria, and Denmark), all hosted by IBT.

For information: International Bicycle Tours, PO Box 754, Essex, CT 06426; 860-767-7005.

VBT BICYCLING VACATIONS

This venerable bike company has recently been acquired by Grand Circle Travel—a specialist in cultural, educational, and adventure vacations around the world for adventurers over the age of 50—and plans to tailor some of VBT's trips for this fast-growing age group. Although challenging routes will remain for those who want them, many of the itineraries in the U.S. and overseas will be less demanding and their schedules more relaxed. As a start, VBT's biking vacations currently include a number of trips eminently suitable for older bikers who seek adventure without all that much physical stress. One is the Salzburg Sojourn, which takes participants on flat bicycle paths and easy descents in the Austrian Alps. Another option is a tour of County Galway and the Connemara Coast in Ireland, visiting small villages, castles and pubs, lush forests, islands, and rocky ocean shores.

For information: VBT, PO Box 711, Bristol, VT 05443; 800-BIKE-TOUR (800-245-3868) or 802-453-4811.

WANDERING WHEELS

A program with a Christian perspective and "a strong biblical orientation," Wandering Wheels operates long-distance bike tours for all ages in this country and abroad, including a 40-day, 2,600-mile Breakaway Coast-to-Coast every spring that's geared specifically for people who are "middle age or older," as are the one-week fall specials that take you to a different locale every year.

For information: Wandering Wheels, PO Box 207, Upland, IN 46989; 765-998-7490.

WOMAN TOURS

Bicycle trips for women are the specialty of this group which schedules at least three trips a year exclusively for women over the age of 50. These trips are selected for their moderate terrain and for mileage that's suitable for both beginning cyclists and more experienced riders. Each a week long, the 50-plus trips this year take you to the California vineyards, the Canadian Rockies from Banff to Jasper, or the Vermont Champlain Valley. A van goes along with every group to carry the luggage and repair equipment and give weary riders a lift. Also for women over 50 is a much more ambitious 56-day, 3,135-mile trip across the entire country, from San Diego, California, to St. Augustine, Florida. Mileage averages 50 to 70 miles a day, mostly on fairly flat terrain, with one rest day per week. For this trip, you'd better be in shape.

For information: Woman Tours, PO Box 68, Coleman Falls, VA 24536; 800-247-1444 or 804-384-7328.

TENNIS, ANYONE?

An estimated three million of the nation's tennis players are over 50, with the number increasing every year as more of us decide to forego rocking chairs for a few fast sets on the courts. You need only a court, a racquet, a can of balls, and an opponent to play tennis, but, if you'd like to be competitive or sociable, you may want to get into some senior tournaments.

UNITED STATES TENNIS ASSOCIATION

The USTA offers a wide variety of tournaments for players over the advanced age of 35, at both local and national levels. To participate, you must be a member ($25 per year). When you join, you will become a member of a regional section, receive periodic schedules of USTA-sponsored tournaments and events in your area for which you can sign up, get a discount on tennis books and publications, and receive a monthly magazine and a free subscription to *Tennis* magazine.

In the schedule of tournaments, you'll find competitions listed for specific five-year age groups: for men from 35 to 85-plus and for women from 35 to 80-plus. There are also self-rated tournaments that match you up with people of all ages who play at your level. If you feel you're good enough to compete, send for an application and sign up. There is usually a modest fee.

For information: USTA, 70 W. Red Oak Lane, White Plains, NY 10604; 914-696-7000.

USTA LEAGUE TENNIS, SENIOR DIVISION

If you want to compete with other 50-plus tennis players in local, area, and sectional competitions on four different surfaces culminating in a national championship, join the Senior Division of the USTA League Tennis program. Your level of play will be rated in a specific skill category ranging from beginner to advanced, and you'll compete only with people on your own ability level. Sign up in your community or write to the USTA for details.

For information: USTA, 70 W. Red Oak Lane, White Plains, NY 10604; 914-696-7000.

USTA PLAY TENNIS AMERICA

The USTA Play Tennis America program is designed to encourage adult beginners, especially those over 50, to learn how to play the game. Available in many communities all over the country in public parks and tennis clubs, this is a three-stage instructional program, with each stage lasting three weeks (three hours a week). You'll learn basic tennis skills and practice playing in low-key competitions.

For information: USTA, 70 W. Red Oak Lane, White Plains, NY 10604-3602; 914-696-7000.

VAN DER MEER TENNIS UNIVERSITY

Van der Meer Tennis University offers five-day Seniors Clinics from September to May every year at its Van der Meer Shipyard Tennis Resort on Hilton Head Island. Specifically for 50-plus players, beginning or experienced, the clinics provide more than 16 hours of instruction, including video analysis, tactics and strategies for singles and doubles, match play drills, plus round robins, social activities, and free court time. The goal is to improve your strokes and game strategy so you'll get more enjoyment out of your game. Discounted accommodations are available for participants. If you attend a clinic on a nonsenior week or weekend, you will get a 10 percent discount by showing your AARP card.

For information: Van der Meer Tennis University, PO Box 5902, Hilton Head Island, SC 29938; 800-845-6138 or 843-785-8388.

WALKING TOURS

There are so many organizations offering walking/hiking trips designed for or eminently suited to mature travelers that we can't list them all here. The following, however, specialize in travel on foot. Other walking trips are mentioned throughout the book. Get yourself in shape for the hikes by walking 10 miles or more every week for at least a month.

APPALACHIAN MOUNTAIN CLUB

Every year this famous hiking club, the oldest conservation and recreation organization in the U.S., schedules a few inexpensive two- to five-day treks especially for people over the age of 50. You'll hike two to eight miles at an easy pace in these lush mountains and valleys and sleep in rustic mountain huts at night, with plenty of time to savor the scenery and glimpse the wildlife. Routes vary from year to year and sometimes include trips for women only. Check out the Silver Sneakers Walking Weekend in New Hampshire in fall foliage season, spring hiking in the White Mountains, and a special traverse of the "high huts."

For information: Appalachian Mountain Club, 5 Joy St., Boston, MA 02108; 617-523-0636.

COMPASS HOLIDAYS

This company specializes in walking and cycling tours in "the heart of the English countryside," the area encompassing the Cotswolds, Bath, Oxford, Cirencester, Tetbury, Stratford, and the Thames Valley. Compass Holidays offers a choice of short holidays with or without the presence of a guide. You'll walk through quiet villages, bustling towns, and pastoral countrysides for three to eight days, covering only a few or many miles, stopping each evening at a small family hotel for local food and a good night's sleep. If you are over the age of 50 and sign up for a minimum of a two-night break, you'll get a 10 percent discount if you mention this book.

For information: Compass Holidays, 48 Shurdington Rd., Cheltenham, Gloucestershire GL53 OJE, UK; +44 (0) 1242-250642; E-mail: compass.holidays@dial.pipex.com.

ELDERHOSTEL BIRDING PROGRAMS

Bird-watchers are in luck, because among Elderhostel's many outdoor programs are overseas trips specifically designed for bird-watching in such countries as Australia, Costa Rica, Ecuador, and Norway. Here in the U.S. there are many Elderhostel programs that include bird-watching among their courses. Study Elderhostel's catalogs for the listings.

For information: Elderhostel, 75 Federal St., Boston, MA 02110; 877-426-8056 or 617-426-7788.

ELDERHOSTEL WALKING & HIKING PROGRAMS

Elderhostel's special international programs include two- or three-week walking and hiking tours for which participants must be regular walkers or hikers in good health. Accompanied by guides, lecturers, and local specialists, the walkers, carrying small day packs, take daily walks ranging from 4 to 12 miles a day, rain or shine. You'll stay and dine mostly in small hotels, while lunch is taken en route. Some of the current destinations are Bermuda, Australia, Austria, Italy, Greece, Norway, South Africa, Wales, England, and Switzerland. Trekking trips are also on Elderhostel's menu, taking you up to eight miles a day on footpaths in Nepal or Argentina. For these you must be in even better physical shape and accustomed to vigorous exercise.

For information: Elderhostel, 75 Federal St., Boston, MA 02110; 877-426-8056 or 617-426-7788.

ELDERTREKS

On these trekking trips in exotic lands, most of them in the Far East, you will hike overland on foot and, in many cases, sleep on an air mattress in a tribal village house or a tent. The trips are rated for difficulty so you may choose one that matches your abilities. For more, see Chapter 5.

For information: ElderTreks, 597 Markham St., Toronto, ON M6G 2L7; 800-741-7956 or 416-588-5000.

50+ MOUNTAIN TOURS

Fully catered and guided camping and hiking tours of the Canadian Rocky Mountains for adventurers over 50 are the specialty of this Canadian company. Starting and ending in Calgary, the tours—7 or 10 days long—are scheduled in the summer months and take a group of no more than eight participants accompanied by four staff members to two campsites, where they settle down in large stand-up tents furnished with comfortable cots. Meals, served up by the cook, are served in a dining tent. Each day, there's a choice of graded hikes, from easy strolls to strenuous all-day hikes deep into the mountains.

For information: 50+ Mountain Tours Ltd., Box 2, Site 3, RR1, Priddis, AB T0L 1W0; 403-931-2208.

INTERHOSTEL

Interhostel's collection of educational trips for people over 50 now includes several walking programs in Bordeaux and the Dordogne Valley of France, another in the Tuscany region of Italy, and others in Scotland and Ireland with more added every year. Moving from place to place by van or bus, you'll set forth on foot to explore, taking leisurely walking tours wherever you go. You'll cover perhaps three to five miles a day, sometimes on unpaved, uneven rocky terrain with stairs and moderate hills, so be sure you are an enthusiastic walker. See Chapter 16 for more about Interhostel programs.

For information: Interhostel, 6 Garrison Ave., Durham, NH 03824; 800-733-9753 or 603-862-1147.

NIFTY OVER FIFTY TOURS

These walking trips in New Zealand, usually scheduled in the spring, allow you to experience city life as well as the rural Maori culture. You can swim with dolphins, cruise overnight on Milford Sound, go whale watching, visit caves, stay overnight on a farm, take tea in a private home, enjoy a Maori feast and concert, and hike in the most scenic areas of the country. Many of the scheduled walks, all optional, are made with local walking clubs and are rated by difficulty and length to suit both ramblers and hikers. The more energetic of the latter are invited to participate in more challenging treks. Options include more days in New Zealand before or after the tour, and stopovers in Australia or on a Pacific island. Horticultural, garden, and bird-watching tours are also offered by this company.

For information: Nifty Over Fifty Tours, Pacific Pathways, 1919 Chula Vista Dr., Belmont, CA 94002; 650-595-2090.

OVERSEAS ADVENTURE TRAVEL

OAT, which runs soft adventure trips all over the globe, has introduced European walking tours designed for the active mature traveler. Everything's included, even airfare, on these leisurely 12- to 14-day guided strolls through Tuscany, the Cotswolds, Ireland, Provence, Scotland, or Switzerland. Rated from easy to challenging, the walks cover three or four miles a day and never exceed seven. Included are extras such as cooking classes, market excursions, painting classes, wine-tasting sessions, and meals in the homes of local residents. See Chapter 3 for more about OAT.

For information: Overseas Adventure Travel, 625 Mt. Auburn St., Cambridge, MA 02138; 800-873-5628 or 617-876-0533.

RIVER ODYSSEYS WEST

If you love wilderness rivers but aren't into whitewater rafting (see Chapter 3), consider ROW's raft-supported walking tours along trails that follow the course of the Middle Fork of the Salmon River in Idaho or the Snake River in Hells Canyon. Carrying only a day pack and led by a guide, you hike six or eight miles a day with plenty of time to smell the flowers and spot the wildlife. A cargo raft carries all the camping gear and your luggage as well as the food and other supplies, and a smaller support raft floats along at the group's pace to act as a sag wagon for tired walkers. When you arrive at camp each afternoon, the staff has already set up the roomy tents and the kitchen and has started cooking dinner, giving you time to relax, fish, or explore.

For information: River Odysseys West, PO Box 579-UD, Coeur d'Alene, ID 83816; 800-451-6034 or 208-765-0841.

SHOTT'S WALKS IN THE WEST

On these guided walking trips exclusively for people over the age of 50, you'll explore places you'd never see from a car or a bus, have close encounters with the scenic West, get your exercise, and have time left over for sight-seeing and shopping. But you won't be spending the nights in a sleeping bag under the stars—you'll sleep in a comfortable bed in a lodge or a motel, complete with bathroom. Recent walks have taken place in Arches and Canyonlands National Parks and Saguaro National Park.

Trips are limited to six guests per guide and you carry only your own day pack. If you can walk comfortably for about 10 miles a week, you're in shape for these hikes.

For information: Shott's Walks in the West, PO Box 51106, Colorado Springs, CO 80949; 719-531-9577.

SILVER SNEAKER EXCURSIONS

Exclusively for people over 50, Silver Sneaker walking tours are guided by experienced Appalachian Mountain Club leaders Linda Cooper and Dick Yeaw. In the U.S., their trips vary from weekends to 18-day adventures, including hikes from inn to inn in Vermont; or walks on Rhode Island's beaches, in Sedona and the Grand Canyon in Arizona,

on the coast of Maine in foliage season, and around the famous resort city of Newport, Rhode Island. Abroad, they
offer hiking trips in Wales or England's Cornwall as well as
the Copper Canyon in Mexico.

See Chapter 14 for this company's ski adventures.

For information: Silver Sneaker Excursions, 100 Worsley
Ave., N. Kingstown, RI 02852; 401-295-0367.

WALK YOUR WAY

Walk Your Way Into the Heart of England tours are led by
Rosemary Davenport Quick in her native land and always
include a few trips per year for older walkers. These are 12-
day tours off the beaten path in quaint and picturesque
places on the Isle of Wight, the Lake District, the Dales of
Yorkshire, or the Cotswolds. Some walks are circular, beginning and ending in the same village, averaging 5 miles
a day. Others are linear, covering 8 to 10 miles a day. The
group is never larger than 10, lodging is in family guest
houses or B&Bs, and evening meals are eaten in a local pub.
For information: Walk Your Way, PO Box 231, Red Feather
Lakes, CO 80545; 970-881-2709.

WALKING THE WORLD

Anyone over 50 who loves adventure and is in good physical shape is invited to participate in Walking the World's
explorations. These are 7- to 17-day back-country treks,
covering 6 to 10 miles a day, that focus on natural and cultural history. On some trips, you'll camp out and, carrying
only a day pack, hike to each new destination. On others,
you will lodge in cabins, small country inns, or B&Bs, set-

ting forth on daily walks into the countryside. Groups are small, from 12 to 18 participants plus two local guides, and there's no upper age limit. No previous hiking experience is necessary.

Destinations include Arches and Canyonlands National Parks in Utah; Banff and Jasper National Parks in the Canadian Rockies; plus trips in Maine, Arizona, Scotland, England, Wales, Switzerland, Ireland, Portugal, New Zealand, Hawaii, Tahiti, Peru, Ecuador, Costa Rica, and Italy.

For information: Walking the World, PO Box 1186, Fort Collins, CO 80522; 800-340-9255 or 498-225-0500.

EXPLORING BY SNOWMOBILE
SENIOR WORLD TOURS

Explore the winter wonders of the Tetons and Yellowstone National Park on your own snowmobile on a seniors-only two- or four-day adventure trip planned by Senior World Tours. Included in the package are driving lessons, snowmobiles, fuel, boots, gloves, helmets, cross-country skis, breakfasts, dinners, and an experienced guide. No experience is necessary, but don't even think of going unless you enjoy the outdoors and the snow and are in good physical condition. Starting at Togwatee, 50 miles out of Jackson, Wyoming, you'll ride through Yellowstone and Gros Ventre River Valley to view the wildlife, geysers, hot springs, and splendid scenery. Every year, by the way, there are a couple of tours for "ladies only."

For information: Senior World Tours, 2205 N. River Rd., Fremont, OH 43420; 888-355-1686.

SNOWSHOEING
APPALACHIAN MOUNTAIN CLUB
In addition to its hiking trips, AMC, a leader in backcountry and environmental education, mountain ecology, and river research, offers a couple of three-day weekend snowshoe adventures for over-50s—one for beginners, the other for intermediates. You can try new skills and practice old ones while you explore the forests. You must be in good shape and capable of carrying a full day pack, including food.

For information: Appalachian Mountain Club, 5 Joy St., Boston, MA 02108; 617-523-0636.

MOTORCYCLE HEAVEN
BEACH'S MOTORCYCLE ADVENTURES
If motorcycling is your passion and adventure is in your blood, look into motorcycle tours offered by the Beaches, a family that's been conducting cycling tours since 1972. All ages, including yours, may choose among several itineraries including the Alpine Adventure through the mountains of Germany, Austria, Italy, Switzerland, and France; the Maori Meander in the backcountry of New Zealand; and the Viking Vector along the Norwegian coast. Motorcycles, all BMWs, are provided in your choice of available models and there is no mileage charge. Your luggage is carried by a van. By the way, both bikes and automobiles are welcome on these tours, so if friends or family want to join you they may go along in a car.

You're on your own during the day, following a tour book that gives daily itineraries, road maps, distances, estimated en route times, business hours, sight-seeing ideas, good (and bad) roads, suggestions for activities, driving tips, and directions to the hotel of the night. The daily routing, pace, and stops are up to you. There are several riding options for each day, so you may decide to cruise along or ride long and hard. Every evening, however, you'll meet the group and your guide at a comfortable hotel or family farm where you'll eat dinner that night and have breakfast the next morning.

For information: Beach's Motorcycle Adventures, 2763 W. River Parkway, Grand Island, NY 14072; 716-773-4960.

RETREADS MOTORCYCLE CLUB

Retreads, an association of motorcycle enthusiasts who have reached the ripe old age of at least 40, get together for state, regional, and international rallies to talk cycling and ride together. Each state association also schedules weekly or monthly gatherings. Started as a correspondence club in 1969, it has grown to over 15,000 members—men and women—in the U.S., Canada, and several other countries including Japan, England, and Australia. Annual contribution is $15 a year per person or $20 per couple. A club newsletter keeps members informed of the activities.

For information: Retreads Motorcycle Club International, 528 North Main St., Albany, IN 47320; 765-789-4070. From November 1 to May 31: 4504 Pittenger Dr., Sarasota, FL 34234; 941-351-7199.

CANOE VACATIONS
GUNFLINT NORTHLAND OUTFITTERS

These outfitters, with paddling adventures on the remote lakes of the Boundary Waters Wilderness Area between Minnesota and Ontario, the largest waterways wilderness in the world, schedule several one-week trips every summer expressly for seniors. With a guide, you paddle and portage your canoe deep into heavily forested areas, home to moose, beaver, mink, loons, and other creatures of the wild. One option is a seven-night package limited to eight guests that includes two nights at Gunflint Lodge and five nights camping with complete outfitting. Camp is set up for you, and your meals—perhaps including the fish you've caught—are cooked over the campfire by your guide. The second choice is a lodge-to-lodge trip that combines three nights at the lodge, one night at a rustic inn on an island across the border in Canada, and the others exploring and camping in the wilderness. Yet another option is gathering a few friends and setting up your own special trip.

For information: Gunflint Northland Outfitters, 750 Gunflint Trail, Grand Marais, MN 55604; 800-362-5251.

KAYAKING TOURS
NEW ZEALAND ADVENTURES

Here's your chance to take a five-day sea kayak tour among the six main islands in the Bay of Islands in New Zealand. This is a relaxed tour specifically for you and your peers over 50, and the only criteria for participation is that you are in good health and enjoy an active vacation. You'll stay in a cabin in Otehei Bay on Urupukapuka Island, eat home-cooked meals, and travel with a knowledgeable local kayak guide your own age. You'll paddle two to four miles a day by kayak exploring the volcanic rock formations and sea caves, take day hikes on island trails, swim, snorkel, sail, and become acquainted with the Maori culture. Trips are scheduled in our winter, New Zealand's summer. For more vigorous tent camping adventures, join a tour "for all ages." *For information:* New Zealand Adventures, HCR 56 Box 575, John Day, OR 97845; 541-932-4925.

GOLFING VACATIONS

GREENS FEES

Most municipal and many private golf courses offer senior golfers (usually those over 65) a discount off the regular greens fees. Take your identification with you and always make inquiries before you play.

GOLF ACADEMY OF HILTON HEAD ISLAND

Golfers over 50 will get a 15 percent discount on the three-day golf schools at the Golf Academy of Hilton Island at Sea Pines if they mention this book when they make their reservations. The school includes five hours of daily instruction from Class A PGA professionals each morning, followed by 18 holes of golf each afternoon. Also included are on-course instruction, video analysis with a take-home tape, a personalized improvement manual, plus breakfast and lunch all three days.
For information: Golf Academy of Hilton Head Island, PO Box 5580, Hilton Head Island, SC 29938; 800-925-0467 or 803-785-4540.

THE GOLF CARD

Designed especially for senior golfers, the Golf Card entitles members to two complimentary rounds of golf per year per course at over 1,600 courses in the country, up to half off the player's fees at 1,800 additional courses, and savings at 300 golf resorts in the U.S., Canada, the Bahamas, Jamaica, and the Dominican Republic. Current membership fees are $75 the first year for a single or $120 for a couple, thereafter $70 a year for a single and $110 for a couple. A subscription to *Golf Traveler*, a magazine that serves as a guide to the participating courses and resorts, is part of the package.

For information: The Golf Card, PO Box 7022, Englewood, CO 80155; 800-321-8269 or 303-790-2267.

NATIONAL SENIOR SPORTS ASSOCIATION (NSSA)

More than 3,000 golfers over 50—average age 63—belong to NSSA, which sponsors recreational and competitive four-day midweek golf holidays once or twice a month at highly rated courses all over the country. The holidays include accommodations, golf (including a 54-hole medal-play tournament), breakfasts, at least two dinners, and activities for nonplaying companions. Recent locations have included Pebble Beach Resorts in California; Kings Mill Resort in Williamsburg; Greenbriar in White Sulphur Springs, West Virginia; and Palmilla Resort in Los Cabos, Mexico. Longer golf holidays are scheduled once a year to more far-flung locations such as Ireland and Scotland, Portugal, Canada, and Hawaii.

Membership in NSSA costs $25 a year, includes your spouse, entitles you to participate in the trips, and gets you

a voluminous monthly newsletter. It also includes discounts on travel and selected golf courses around the country.
For information: NSSA, 83 Princeton Ave., Hopewell, NJ 08525; 800-282-6772 or 609-466-0022.

JOHN JACOBS GOLF SCHOOLS

Golfers over the age of 62 get a discount of 10 percent on the cost of golf vacations offered July through December at any John Jacobs Golf School. You'll learn how to improve your game while you play at some of the finest courses in the country. Most packages include lodging, breakfast and dinner, instruction, course time, greens fees, and cart. Commuter packages are available too at all 32 schools.
For information: John Jacobs Golf Schools, 800-472-5007.

EVENTS FOR RAPID RUNNERS
FIFTY-PLUS FITNESS ASSOCIATION

This is not a club, although it occasionally sponsors athletic events for its over-50 members. It is an organization formed by eminent exercise researchers at Stanford University for the exchange of information about physical exercise and its benefits (and hazards) among the older population. Its members, from almost every state and several foreign countries, also serve as volunteers for ongoing studies of such activities as running, swimming, biking, and racewalking. Each is asked to contribute $35 a year, tax-deductible, to defray costs. The association sponsors many events in the California Bay Area. These include walks, runs, swims, bike rides, and seminars and conferences on aging.

For information: Fifty-Plus Fitness Association, PO Box D, Stanford, CA 94309; 650-323-6160.

OVER-50 SOFTBALL

INTERNATIONAL SENIOR SOFTBALL ASSOCIATION

ISSA, an association that was founded to promote softball for men and women over the age of 50, conducts the World Championship Tournaments for over 300 senior teams every year in northern Virginia. Players who are members of senior leagues and local softball associations all over the U.S. may join, and so may individuals without affiliation. Members receive a master nationwide tournament schedule, the results of all national tournaments, and the rankings of all senior softball teams.

For information: ISSA, 9401 East St., Manassas, VA 20110; 703-368-1188.

NATIONAL ASSOCIATION OF SENIOR CITIZEN SOFTBALL

The NASCS is an association of several thousand softball players and hundreds of teams in the U.S. and Canada, with a goal of promoting a worldwide interest in senior softball. To play ball on one of its teams, you must be at least 50 years old. There's no upper age limit, and both men and women are welcomed. NASCS runs about 15 tournaments every year in the U.S. plus one in Canada and is the organizer of the annual Senior Softball World Series, a tournament for players who must first qualify in local competitions. Every year more than 100 teams from the U.S. and Canada compete in a major ballpark. A quarterly magazine keeps members up to date on happenings here and abroad. *For information:* NASCS, PO Box 1085, Mt. Clemens, MI 48046; 810-792-2110.

SENIOR SOFTBALL USA

This organization, the largest senior softball group in the world, conducts softball tournaments all over the country and organizes international tournaments as well, including the Senior Softball World Championship Games held in September. Anyone over 50, man or woman, in the U.S. and Canada may join and many thousands have. Members get assistance finding teams in their areas and may subscribe to the *Senior Softball USA News*, which keeps them up to date on tournaments and other news. They are eligible to take part in an annual international tour that takes teams to play ball in foreign lands.
For information: Senior Softball USA, 7052 Riverside Blvd., Sacramento, CA 95831; 916-393-8566.

SENIOR GAMES

NATIONAL SENIOR GAMES ASSOCIATION

To compete in the national games (formerly known as the U.S. National Senior Olympics) scheduled in a different location every two years, you must first qualify in authorized state competitions. This means you must be a medal winner in your age group or meet minimum performance standards in time and distance events. Sign up now for your state games (call your local senior agency for information) and be ready to join more than 11,000 athletes who will compete in 18 sports next year. Cost is $120 for free access to all event venues and to special events such as social activities, demonstrations, and a ceremony.

For a free list of local and state games all over the country, write to NSGA at the address below. You'll find a representative sample of these games in the following pages. *For information:* NSGA, 445 North Blvd., Ste. 2001, Baton Rouge, LA 70802; 504-379-7337.

HUNTSMAN WORLD SENIOR GAMES

Every October, a few thousand athletes—male and female, 50 and over, from the U.S. and many other countries—gather in St. George, Utah, for two weeks of competition in 29 events from basketball, mountain biking, golf, swimming, and tennis to track and field and triathlon. In addition to athletic events, the games try to foster health, friendship, and world peace through healthy-lifestyle seminars and free health screenings. Included are social events such as receptions, band concerts, and ceremonial dinners. *For information:* Huntsman World Senior Games, 82 W. 700 South, St. George, UT 84770; 800-562-1268 or 435-674-0550.

STATE AND LOCAL SENIOR GAMES

Most states hold their own senior games once or twice a year and send their best competitors to national events. If you don't find your state among those listed here, that doesn't mean there's no program in your area—many are sponsored by counties, cities, even local agencies and colleges. Check with your local city, county, or state recreation departments to see what's going on near you or contact the NSGA for a free list. You don't have to be a serious competitor to enter these games but merely ready to enjoy yourself. So what if you don't go home with a medal? At the very least, you'll meet other energetic people and have a lot of laughs.

ARIZONA

If you are over 50, male or female, you are eligible to participate in the Flagstaff Senior Olympics held over four days every year in September. You may compete in events that include bowling, cycling, golf, handball, racewalking, swimming, tennis, track and field, powerlifting, and more. Sign up for the festivities, which include an evening social and tickets to a Northern Arizona University football game. Medals are awarded for each event.

For information: Flagstaff Senior Olympics, PO Box 5063, Flagstaff, AZ 86011; 520-523-3560.

CALIFORNIA

Hundreds of senior athletes from all over the world compete for 10 days in February in the annual Palm Springs International Senior Olympics. The sporting events range from track and field to golf and tennis, with medal winners going on to compete in the National Senior Olympics. If you are 50 or more, a resident or a visitor to the state, you are eligible to participate.

For information: Palm Springs International Senior

Olympics, Palm Springs, Mizell Senior Center, 480 S. Sunrise Way, Palm Springs, CA 92262; 760-323-5689.

On the last weekend in February each year, the Running Springs Senior Winter Games are held at a resort in the San Bernardino National Forest. Open to anyone over the age of 50, the competitions include skiing, ice skating, ice fishing, snowball throwing, snowshoe racing, and a few indoor games such as billiards, bridge, and table tennis. Social events are included. There is a modest registration fee plus a small additional fee for each event entered.

For information: Running Springs Senior Winter Games, PO Box 3333, Running Springs, CA 92382; 909-867-3176.

COLORADO

The Senior Winter Games at the Summit take place each year during three days in the second week of February in the quaint Victorian village of Breckenridge. Anyone from anywhere who's over 55 and wants to compete against peers is welcome. Events include cross-country skiing, downhill slalom, speed skating, snowshoe races, biathlon, figure skating, and more, plus social activities. Age categories for the competitions begin at 55 to 59 and increase in five-year increments to 90-plus. A registration fee that allows you to participate in as many events as you wish currently stands at $25.

The summer Rocky Mountain Senior Games are held in Greeley the first week in August and include over 20 competitions in sports ranging from basketball and racquetball to golf, softball, bowling, cycling, and tennis. A registration fee of $41 includes admission to eight different events, continental breakfast, and snacks. To participate, you must be at least 50 and you can compete no matter where you're from.

For information: Senior Winter Games at the Summit, PO Box 442, Breckenridge, CO 80424; 970-453-2461; or Rocky Mountain Senior Games, 1010 6th St., Greeley, CO 80631; 970-350-9433.

CONNECTICUT

The Connecticut Senior Olympics include not only competitive sport events but also a mini health fair and many physical fitness activities. Residents of Connecticut and neighboring states who are 50-plus converge on the town of Southington on the first weekend in June for three days of events such as the 5,000-meter run, the 100-yard dash, the mile run, the long jump, swimming, bocci, and tennis. These summer games require a small entrance fee.

The one-day Connecticut Senior Winter Olympics, held in March, are open to anyone from anywhere who's at least 50 and an amateur. The games feature downhill, giant slalom, cross-country, and snowshoe races, and take place at Ski Sundown.

For information: Connecticut Senior Olympics, PO Box 790, Milldale, CT 06467; 860-621-4661.

FLORIDA

The Golden Age Games in Sanford have taken place every November since 1974. They last for a week and include plenty of competitions, ceremonies, social events, and entertainments. If you are over 55, you are eligible to participate regardless of residency. In other words, you needn't be a Florida resident to compete for the gold, silver, and bronze medals in such sports as basketball, biking, bowling, canoeing, checkers, dance, swimming, tennis, triathlon, track and field, canasta, and croquet. There is a small entry fee for each event.

For information: Golden Age Games, PO Box 1298, Sanford, FL 32772; 407-330-5697.

MICHIGAN

Michigan Senior Olympics, a four-day happening open to people 50 and older, are held every year on the campus of a state college. For small registration and event fees, you get a chance to compete for medals in athletic events from archery to volleyball. You may also take home ribbons for your baking skills, arts and crafts, and dancing. Spectators are welcomed too.

For information: Michigan Senior Olympics, 312 Woodward, Rochester, MI 48307; 810-608-0250.

MISSOURI

The St. Louis Senior Olympics have become an institution in Missouri by now. A four-day event that is open to anyone who lives anywhere and is at least 50 years old, it costs a nominal amount and is action-oriented. No knitting contests here—only energetic events such as bicycle races, 200-meter races, standing long jumps, golf, basketball, free throw, sprints, tennis singles and doubles, and swimming.

For information: Senior Olympics, JCCA, 2 Millstone Campus Dr., St. Louis, MO 63146; 314-432-6780, ext. 3188.

MONTANA

Men and women over the age of 50, from Montana or otherwise, are invited to participate in the Montana Senior Olympics held every year in June. Events range from archery, badminton, bowling, and basketball to swimming, tennis, softball, and track.

For information: Montana Senior Olympics, 3621 Ft. Laramie Ave., Billings, MT 59102; 406-252-2795.

NEW HAMPSHIRE

For three days in September, you can compete with your peers in the Granite State Senior Summer Games, which feature 15 sports events ranging from swimming to tennis, track and field, shuffleboard, and table tennis. In alternate years, these are qualifying games for the U.S. Senior Sports Classic. Sign up if you are at least 50 and in good operating condition. The cost is minimal. Regional games are also scheduled throughout the state during the summer.

The Granite State Senior Winter Games, held in Waterville Valley for three days in March, are open to men and women 50 and over who compete in groups of five-year increments. They get a chance to challenge their peers in dual slalom, giant slalom, and cross-country races. Other events include speed skating, snowball throw, hockey goal shoot, and snowshoe races. Everyone in the appropriate age range is welcome to enter the competitions and attend both an opening reception and an awards banquet. Costs for entry, lift tickets, fees, rentals, and social affairs are low. Inexpensive lodging is also available.

For information: Granite State Senior Winter Games, PO Box 1942, Rochester, NH 03866; 603-332-0055.

NEW JERSEY

Held in June, the New Jersey Senior Sports Classic games usually feature more than 1,000 seniors competing in 21 competitive sports such as archery, golf, basketball, softball, tennis, and track and field.

For information: Senior Citizens Activities Network, Monmouth Mall, Eatontown, NJ 07724; 732-542-1326.

NEW YORK

The Empire State Senior Games, open to all New York residents who are 50 or over, are held in Syracuse over three days in June. Winners may qualify for the National Senior Olympics. For a small registration fee, amateur athletes may compete in many events that range from swimming to bridge, basketball, softball, croquet, track and field, tennis, racewalking, cycling, and more. There are additional fees for golf and bowling. Participants are invited to social events each of the three nights.

For information: Empire State Senior Games, NYS Parks, 6105 E. Seneca Turnpike, Jamesville, NY 13078; 315-492-9654.

NORTH CAROLINA

After local games are held statewide, the winners travel to Raleigh for the North Carolina Senior Games State Finals and, perhaps, on to the national games. Most sports are on the agenda, plus an arts competition that celebrates artists in heritage, literary, performing, and visual arts. The state also sponsors the SilverStriders, a walking club for those 50 or better that gives its members logbooks for tracking progress, gifts and awards, and an annual report of their accomplishments.

For information: North Carolina Senior Games, PO Box 33590, Raleigh, NC 27636; 919-851-5456.

PENNSYLVANIA

The Keystone Senior Games "combine sports, recreation, and entertainment with fellowship." You can get some of each if you are a Pennsylvania resident who is 50 or older. The games are held over five days in July at a university campus where you can get lodging and three meals a day at low cost. If you prefer to stay in a motel, you'll get a senior discount.

For information: Keystone Senior Games, 31 S. Hancock St., Wilkes Barre, PA 18702; 717-823-3164.

VERMONT

If you are over 50 and an amateur in your sport, you are invited to participate in the Green Mountain Senior Games. At the summer games held in September at Green Mountain College in Poultney, the competitive events—organized in age groups from 50 to 95-plus—include everything from golf and tennis to swimming, darts, horseshoes, walking, running, table tennis, bowling, croquet, softball, basketball, and mountain biking. And just for fun, there are scenic walks, socials, and free swims. A fee of $15 covers everything including lunch.

For information: Green Mountain Senior Games, 131 Holden Hill Rd., Weston, VT 05161; 802-824-6521.

VIRGINIA

The Virginia Senior Games are an annual four-day event held each spring on a college campus, where older athletes

compete to qualify for the U.S. National Senior Olympics—
or just for the fun of it. It is a combination of social events
and entertainment with sports competitions, open to Virginia residents over the age of 50. Spouses are invited to
come along and enjoy the hospitality, which includes parties, dances, tours of local sites, and other festivities. The
fees are low, lodging and meals are cheap, and the sporting
events are many, ranging from rope jumping, miniature
golf, and riflery to swimming, running, and tennis for age
groups from 55 upwards.

For information: Virginia Senior Games, Virginia Recreation
and Park Society, 6038 Cold Harbor Rd., Mechanicsville,
VA 23111; 804-730-9447.

14

Adventures on Skis

OVER THE TOP

Downhill skiing is one sport you'd think would appeal only to less mature, less wise, less breakable people. On the contrary, there is an astounding number of ardent over-50 skiers who would much rather glide down mountains than sit around waiting for springtime. In fact, many of us ski more than ever now that we're older because we can go midweek when the crowds are thinner and we get impressive discounts on lift tickets. And a lot of us are taking up the sport for the first time. Ski schools all over the United States and Canada are reporting an increase of older students in beginner classes.

The truth is, you're never too old to learn how to ski or to improve your technique. Once you get the hang of it, you can ski at your own speed, choosing the terrain, the difficulty level, and the challenge. You can swoop down cliffs through narrow icy passes or wend your way on gentle slopes in a more leisurely fashion, aided by the new improved skis and boots, clearly marked and carefully groomed trails, and sophisticated lifts that take all the work out of getting up the mountain.

Besides, ski resorts are falling all over themselves catering to older skiers, offering discounts on lift tickets, cheaper season passes, and other engaging incentives. In fact, it is a rare ski area that does not give a substantial break to skiers over a certain age.

CLUBS FOR MATURE SKIERS
OVER THE HILL GANG

If you are sociable and cost-conscious, consider signing up for a ski club such as the Over the Hill Gang (see Chapter 13). This club, which you can join at age 50, schedules a wide assortment of escorted ski trips every year in this country and abroad. Members—about 6,500 to date—are entitled to senior discounts, usually available only to skiers much older than 50, at many of the top ski areas.

The club's 11 regional "gangs," or chapters, run their own ski trips as well, and all members everywhere are invited to go along. At some ski areas, local and visiting members meet regularly to ski together with their own guides. At Steamboat and Copper Mountain, in Colorado, for example, they gather four days a week during the season. At Vail, they ski together on Mondays; at Breckenridge on Tuesdays; Winter Park on Wednesdays; and at Keystone on Thursday mornings. Out-of-town members and anyone else over 50 are invited to come along.

Members who reach their 70th birthday (and are willing to admit it) are part of the "Over 70 Gang," and members who have turned 80 are included in the "Over 80 Gang." They receive special shoulder patches and a discount on their next membership renewal or their next trip with the club.

When ski season ends, you may join OTHG for other activities including biking, rafting, hiking, and golfing.

Annual membership fee: $40 single, $65 per couple, plus chapter dues if you join a local chapter.

For information: Over the Hill Gang International, 1820 W. Colorado Ave., Dept. G., Colorado Springs, CO 80904; 719-389-0022.

70+ SKI CLUB

Once you hit 70, you're eligible to join the 70+ Ski Club for an annual fee of $10 ($15 for couples)—until you're 90, when it's free. Don't laugh. Among the approximately 14,000 current members worldwide, 174 are over the age of 90 and almost 4,000 are between 80 and 90. Members get a selection of ski trips and special events every year at ski resorts in the Northeast and the West; at least one in Europe; and the others in New Zealand, Chile, or Argentina. Hunter Mountain in New York hosts the club's annual meeting each March. Here the 70+ Ski Races have become such a popular event that contestants are divided into three age groups: men 70 to 80, women 70 to 80, and anyone over 80. Awards are presented at a gala party at the lodge.

Founded in 1977, the club has always promoted the interests of senior skiers, especially those on limited incomes. Today, largely as a result of its efforts, most ski areas give seniors free or half-price lift tickets.

Proof of age is required with your application to join the club, and you may not apply earlier than two weeks before your 70th birthday. Members receive a patch, a membership card, a periodic newsletter, and a directory of areas around the country that offer discounts or free skiing.
For information: 70+ Ski Club, 1633 Albany St., Schenectady, NY 12304; 518-346-5505.

SILVER SNEAKER EXCURSIONS

Anybody over 50 is invited to join Silver Sneaker Excursions for a weekend or longer of downhill skiing, cross-country, and/or snowshoeing in New Hampshire or Vermont. Featured are small groups, instruction if you need it, all kinds of terrain, sometimes skiing door to door from inn to inn.
For information: Silver Sneaker Excursions, 100 Worsley Ave., N. Kingstown, RI 02852; 401-295-0367.

THE WILD OLD BUNCH

Skiers who frequent Alta in Utah are advised to search out members of the Wild Old Bunch, an informal group of long-time skiers who hang out together on the mountain and welcome anyone who wants to join them. There are no rules, no regulations, no meetings. The only requirement is that you must be over 55. The group grows haphazardly as members pick up stray mature skiers on the slopes. Lunch is usually on the deck of the mid-mountain Alpenglow Inn.

For information: Look for the Wild Old Bunch on the slopes.

GOOD DEALS EVERYWHERE FOR SKIERS

The older you are, the less it costs to ski. There's hardly a ski area in North America today that doesn't give mature skiers a good deal. Many cut the price of lift tickets in half for skiers at age 65, and most stop charging altogether at 70, although a couple—Alta in Utah and Mt. Tom in Massachusetts—make you wait until you're 80 to ski free. A few areas charge anybody over the age of 65 only $5 a day for lift tickets, and most make offers on season passes that are hard to refuse. Others plan special senior programs specifically for mature skiers.

To give you an idea of what's out there, here is a sampling of the special senior programs, workshops, and clubs in the states where skiing is big business. This list does not include all areas, of course, so be sure to check out others in locations that interest you. Remember to carry proof of age with you at all times. The ski areas change their programs every year or so, too; so, using the following information as a guide, you must do some of your own research.

CALIFORNIA

Ski in California and you'll get good deals on lift tickets and season passes almost everywhere. Plus, there are some special programs designed especially for mature skiers, such as the following.

Tahoe Donner Downhill Ski Area schedules ski clinics for skiers over the age of 50 every Tuesday morning.

The inexpensive package for beginners and experienced skiers includes a lift ticket, continental breakfast, three hours of ski lessons, and a videotape review of your skiing technique.

At Northstar-at-Tahoe, the three-day Golden Stars Clinic has been tailored for skiers over 60 of intermediate or better ability who want to improve their skills on the slopes. Offered several times a winter, the clinic provides daily three-hour lessons and all-day lift tickets.

At Heavenly Ski Resort, there are free four-hour workshops for skiers over 55. And Mammoth Mountain offers three-day senior ski clinics.

The senior program at Bear Valley, in the Sierra Nevada Mountains between Lake Tahoe and Yosemite, is even better. At 65, you may ski free any day, any time. If you prefer a season pass, you can get one for just $10.

COLORADO

Every ski area in Colorado offers discounted lift tickets to seniors, some starting at 60, others at 65, and every ski area charges nothing at all to ski after 70. And there are many special programs, lessons, and clubs especially designed for mature skiers. For example:

At Breckenridge, two-day Silver Seminars for skiers over 50 of all abilities, taught by seniors, include lift tickets, lessons, video analysis, and a group dinner. Breckenridge is the place where members of the local Over the Hill Gang, plus any other visitors 50 and over, get together on Tuesdays for a day on the slopes with their own guide. Breckenridge also hosts the Senior Winter Games at the Summit for three days in February.

It's Thursday mornings at Keystone for Gang members and visitors to ski with volunteer guides.

At Vail, any skier over 50 is welcome to meet on Mondays and ski with OTHG members. At Steamboat, together with volunteer guides, they gang up on the slopes every day from Sunday through Thursday. At Copper Mountain, they usually meet four days a week and take part in ski clinics and social events. At all of the mountains, all 50-plus skiers, members or not, are invited along.

Silver Creek Resort offers Never-Ever 50+, a learn-to-ski program exclusively for mature people who have never been on skis before. Scheduled on Wednesday and Saturday mornings, it includes lesson, equipment, and lift ticket.

Sunlight Mountain Resort in Glenwood Springs has its 100 Club, open to couples whose combined ages total 100 years or more, or singles who are 50 or older. Club members meet each Wednesday to ski in the morning and stay for lunch.

Powderhorn's New Tricks for Old Dogs is a program that meets on four Thursdays a year during ski season to help older skiers improve their techniques and learn how to use the new-shaped skis. Included are a personal video analysis and a farewell party.

Crested Butte Mountain, too, has one-day senior workshops for beginners to advanced skiers, and a senior women's group called the Crested Butte Beauties welcomes visitors and locals. At Eldora, skiers and snowboarders 65 and older can participate in Senior Ski every Tuesday. Senior Days at Ski Cooper gives you a day lift ticket, free racing and an après-ski party. Telluride's Master Club race program for seniors meets on Saturdays for lessons on gate training, carving techniques, and speed.

The SnoMasters Classic at Purgatory, for skiers 55 and over, is a four-day event held twice every winter, providing discounted lessons by instructors of your own generation, breakfast each morning, and a party.

At Winter Park Resort, the Ski Meisters ski three days a week with volunteer guides. With 400 members and a waiting list, the club charges a one-time fee of $100, then $50 a year. To keep themselves busy when ski season is over, members gather for biking, hiking, tennis, and golf vacations.

The Ski Forever Week at Telluride in February caters to mature skiers, from beginners to experts. It includes five hours a day of on-snow instruction, video analysis, evening seminars, an afternoon at a spa, social gatherings, and a farewell party.

IDAHO

Sun Valley's Prime Time Special, a week reserved for older skiers, is scheduled twice each winter. It includes lodging for seven nights, daily lift tickets, discount coupons, races, special events, and a Big Band Buffet Dinner Dance.

Schweitzer Mountain's Prime Timers Club for skiers 55 and over is an informal club whose members ski together almost every day and get together for social gatherings every Thursday afternoon. In addition, there's a bargain senior ski week in March, the Snowmaster's Classic, a week of workshops, clinics, social activities, and race training for older skiers who are seeking to improve their technical abilities.

MAINE

At Sunday River Ski Resort, those who purchase the Perfect Turn Gold Card or Platinum Card and are 50 or over are eligible for unlimited membership in the Prime Time Club. The club skis together with an instructor for two hours every Saturday and Sunday morning. The cards also entitle participants to discounts on private ski clinics.

At Sugarloaf/USA, a Perfect Turn Gold or Platinum Card is what you need to participate free in the Prime Time Club for skiers over 50. This card is good for group skiing and coaching once a week.

MASSACHUSETTS

Jiminy Peak in Hancock holds Senior Day every Thursday, when, if you already have a season pass or are over 70, the cost is only $20 for a lift ticket and a two-hour ski clinic. For others, the day costs twice as much.

At Catamount, members of the 70+ Club ski for $7 any time.

MICHIGAN

Every Tuesday in January and February, except holidays, is Silver Streak Day at Crystal Mountain Resort. Here, if you are 55 or more, you're entitled to free group lessons, 50 percent off rental equipment, and an all-day lift ticket.

NEVADA

At Mt. Rose, just outside of Reno, skiers over 50 are welcomed every Friday morning for coffee and a free two-hour mountain clinic with senior instructors.

NEW HAMPSHIRE

It's a rare ski area in this state that does not offer older skiers an impressive break on lift tickets at age 65 or so and a free pass at 70. Many also have special programs for senior skiers.

If you're 55 or older you can join the Silver Streaks at Waterville Valley, paying only $2 a day or $50 for the season plus the price of lift tickets to ski the slopes with a guide four mornings a week. If you are 65, it costs you only $10 a day midweek for your lift ticket. Cross-country skiers who join Silver Streaks may ski with a guide at the Nordic Center on Wednesdays for $10 per session or $50 for the season.

At Attitash Bear Peak, members of TGIF (Thank Goodness I'm Fifty) get 14 weeks of two-hour group lessons on Thursday mornings, plus other perks such as breakfast, workshops, and a party for only $5 a day or $50 for the season plus the price of midweek lift tickets.

At Loon Mountain, Flying 50s Plus meets every Thursday and Friday morning except on holidays for two-hour group skiing. Members also get discounts on lift tickets, lodging, and special activities.

At Cannon Mountain, Senior Cruises, for skiers over 50, meets Monday mornings to ski for two hours with instructors.

At Gunstock, Mountain Meisters, for over-50 skiers, meets every Thursday for skills clinics and video analysis. Special events include a recreational race day.

At Temple Mountain, the Morning Birds, a seven-week program for seniors, runs Monday through Friday with lessons on skiing or snowboarding.

In January at King Pine Ski Area at Purity Spring Resort, skiers over 50 get five days of free lessons in alpine or cross-country skiing or snowboarding. Reservations are required.

Ragged Mountain offers its Mountain Ramblers ski club for skiers over 50, who meet on Tuesday mornings for a group lesson.

NEW MEXICO

Sign up for a Masters Ski Week at Taos Ski Valley and you get six mornings of instruction, all-day lift tickets for the week, and après-ski seminars.

NEW YORK

Skiers over 50 are invited to join the Senior Skier Development Program at Ski Windham for eight weeks on Tuesdays from January to March. You may attend the program by the day, if you prefer. What you get is morning coffee, presentations on ski-related subjects, morning and afternoon on-snow lessons, and lunch.

PENNSYLVANIA

At Blue Knob Four Seasons Resort in Claysburg, skiers over 65 pay junior rates any time, and those over 70 ski free midweek.

UTAH

Virtually all of Utah's ski areas give senior skiers reduced rates on lift tickets at 60 or 65, with Sundance and Elk

Meadows offering free rides to those over 65. Most others stop charging at 70—except Alta, where you must wait until you are 80!

Junior's Seniors, for which you qualify at age 62, meets at Snowbird on Tuesday mornings. Members ski free for three hours with well-known ski instructor Junior Bounous. For $20 plus the price of a lift ticket, they can then return to the slopes for the afternoon and work on what they've learned.

Alta's ski school gives special three-hour Silver Meisters lessons on Fridays and Sundays designed specifically for mature skiers who want to improve their skills.

The seniors program at Sundance sets aside four afternoon sessions a month for group skiing with a guide.

As for Brighton Ski Resort, the Senior Workshop, held on three consecutive weeks for skiers of all levels over 50, includes lessons, a lift pass, breakfast, and a social hour.

VERMONT

Vermont's ski areas were the first to cater to older skiers, and it is highly unlikely that there are any resorts there that don't give seniors a decent break on lift tickets and season passes. Along with special rates, several areas offer special senior programs as well. Here's a sample.

At Jay Peak any skier over the age of 55 is invited to join the Silver Peaks Club, a group that skis together every Tuesday. For a nominal fee, you are entitled to a day that includes your lift ticket, guide, coffee and doughnuts, and après-ski activities. If you're over 65, you may ski here any time for $10 a day.

The Silver Griffins Senior Program at Bromley Mountain meets every nonholiday Monday and Tuesday for group skiing, fun races, picnics, and parties. Members of the group get preferred parking midweek and discounts on food, equipment, and lessons.

For a fee of $10 for the season, Smuggler's Notch offers its Smuggler's 55-Plus Club which meets on Wednesdays for breakfast, morning skiing with a guide, and afternoon activities such as movies, demonstrations, and guest speakers. Members also get half off the cost of lift tickets, rentals, and group lessons.

15

Back to Summer Camp

Maybe you thought camp was just for kids, but if you are a grown-up person who likes the outdoors, swimming, boating, birds, and arts and crafts and appreciates fields and forests and star-filled skies, you too can pack your bags and go off on a sleepaway. Throughout the country, many camps set aside weeks for adult sessions, while others offer adult programs all season long. More and more adults are getting hooked on summer camp, and many wouldn't miss a year.

ELDERHOSTEL

Many of Elderhostel's programs are a combination of camping and college. In this wildly successful low-cost educational program (see Chapter 16 for details), you can spend a week or two camping in remote scenic areas, enjoying all the activities from horseback riding to crafts, boating, campfires, and sleeping in a cabin or under the stars. *For information:* Elderhostel, 75 Federal St., Boston, MA 02110; 617-426-7788. In Canada: Elderhostel Canada, 5 Cataraqui St., Kingston, ON K7K 1Z7; 613-530-2222.

RV ELDERHOSTELS

On these Elderhostels, you take along your own housing— a recreational vehicle, travel trailer, or tent—and stay on the host campus or at a nearby campgrounds. Classes, usually held on the campus, are included, as are meals and excursions. On most RV tours you join the group for classes, meals, and excursions, but sleep on your own premises. On others, a group of RVers form a moving field trip, moving along like a wagon train, listening to lectures over their CB radios as they travel and making stops along the way. *For information:* Elderhostel, 75 Federal St., Boston, MA 02110; 877-426-8056 or 617-426-7788.

GRANDPARENTS/GRANDCHILDREN CAMP

See Chapter 3 for information about summer camps and other vacations designed to give grandparents and grandchildren some special time together.

THE SALVATION ARMY

The Salvation Army operates scores of rural camps across the country, most of which have year-round adult sessions. The camps are run by regional divisional headquarters of the army; thus each is different from the others. Open to anyone, they cost very little.
For information: Contact a local unit of the Salvation Army.

VOLUNTARY ASSOCIATION FOR SENIOR CITIZEN ACTIVITIES

VASCA is a nonprofit organization that will provide you with detailed information about camps in the New York area for people over the age of 55. The agency represents 11 vacation lodges scattered about New York, New Jersey, Connecticut, and Pennsylvania, all of them amazingly affordable. Some are small rustic country retreats, most are lakeside resorts, others are huge sprawling complexes with endless activities. Several are designed to accommodate the disabled and the blind as well as the very elderly. The camps are sponsored by various nonprofit organizations and foundations, some with religious affiliations but nonsectarian.

For information: VASCA, 281 Park Ave. South, New York, NY 10010; 212-645-6590.

YMCA/YWCA

The Y runs many camps, most of them for children, but some also offer inexpensive weeks for adults. For example, the YMCA of the Rockies operates a resort, Snow Mountain Ranch, with a special program in mid-August for active adults over the age of 50 at its Camp Chief Ouray in Granby, Colorado. The High Point YMCA's Camp Cheerio in the Appalachian Mountains of North Carolina sets aside three weeks a year for campers over 50, who live in the same cabins and pursue the same activities as the kids do the rest of the summer.

For information: Call your local YMCA or YWCA for information about camps in your area.

CAMPS SPONSORED BY CHURCH GROUPS

There are many adult camps and summer workshops sponsored by religious organizations, too many and too diverse to list here. One source of information is Christian Camping International, which sells a guide listing over 900 camps and conferences in the U.S.

For information: Christian Camping International/USA, PO Box 62189, Colorado Springs, CO 80962; 719-260-9400.

16

Going Back to School After 50

Have you always wanted to learn French, study African birds, examine Eskimo culture, learn to paddle a canoe or ski down a mountain, delve into archaeology, international finance, horticulture, the language of whales, or great literature of the 19th century? Now is the time to do it. If you're a typical member of the over-50 generation, you're in good shape, healthy and alert, with the energy and the time to pursue new interests. So why not go back to school and learn all those things you've always wished you knew?

You are welcome as a regular student at just about any institution in the United States and Canada, especially in the continuing-education programs, but many colleges and universities have set up special programs designed to lure older people back to the classroom. Some offer good reductions in tuition (so good indeed that often you may attend regular classes at half price or even free) and give credits for life experience. Others have designed programs, and sometimes whole schools, specifically for mature scholars.

Going back to class is an excellent way to generate feelings of accomplishment and to exercise the mind—and one of the best ways to make new friends. It doesn't necessarily mean you'll have to turn in term papers or take excruciatingly difficult exams. Sign up for one class a week on flower arranging or Spanish conversation or a once-a-month lecture series on managing your money. Or register as a part-time or full-time student in a traditional university program. Or take a learning vacation on a college campus. Do it *your* way.

You don't even have to attend classes to learn on vacation. You can go on archaeological digs, count butterflies, help save turtles from extinction, brush up on your bassoon playing, listen to opera, search for Roman remains in Europe, study dancing or French cuisine, or go on safari in Africa.

BOARDWALK U.

Located at the Port-O-Call Hotel on the boardwalk in Ocean City near Atlantic City on the Jersey shore, Boardwalk U. is designed for seniors. It features a low-cost, five-day educational vacation program that includes four nights of lodging, all meals, a choice of two two-hour classes a day from over 50 courses taught by professional instructors, and a gala "graduation lunch." Offered nine months of the year (excluding the summer), courses range from Bible study to basic bridge, Shakespeare, needle arts, children's literature, legal guidance for seniors, Chinese history, hypnotism,

Spanish, and computers. Evenings are open for socializing and entertainment.

For information: Boardwalk U., Port-O-Call Hotel, 1510 Boardwalk, Ocean City, NJ 08226; 800-334-4546 or 609-399-8812.

CHAUTAUQUA INSTITUTION

For over a century people have been traveling up to the shores of Lake Chautauqua, in southwestern New York State, to a cultural summer center set in a Victorian village. The 856-acre hilltop complex offers a wide variety of educational programs, including summer weeks and off-season weekends designed for people over the age of 55. The 55-Plus Weekends and the Residential Week for Older Adults are filled up far in advance, so if you are interested, don't waste a moment before signing up.

Each 55-Plus Weekend has a specific focus, such as the U.S. Constitution, natural history, national politics, music

A WEEK IN THE MOUNTAINS

An annual six-day program every fall geared to the over-50 set, **Explore** offers symposia, workshops, and clinics in fields from history, music, and astronomy to photography, gourmet cooking, crafts, and fly-fishing; plus, there are guest speakers, fitness classes, and social activities.

For information: Explore, NorthStar Institute, 312 S. Franklin St., Denver, CO 80209; 800-298-4242 or 303-777-6873.

appreciation, or trade relations with Japan. They include discussions, workshops, lectures, films, recreational activities, and evening entertainment, all led by professionals.

Housing and meals are available in a residence hall with double rooms and shared baths.

The Residential Week for Older Adults is similar but longer and includes lodging and meals as well as admittance to other happenings at the center.

It's all quite cheap. The cost of tuition, room, meals, and planned activities for a Residential Week is currently $475, while a 55-Plus Weekend costs $40 for commuters or $140 if you want accommodations and meals.

For information: Program Center for Older Adults, Chautauqua, NY 14722; 800-836-ARTS or 716-357-6200.

CLOSE UP WASHINGTON

For an insider's view of Washington, D.C., and the federal government, you can attend classes on current events, study the presidents, exchange views with national political leaders, and gain insights on public policy, all in a tightly packed week of on-site seminars organized for older adults by the Close Up Foundation. What's more, there's time for relaxation, conversation, social events, theater, and exploration in the nation's capital.

Offering a choice of about a dozen one-week programs a year in cooperation with AARP, Close Up uses Washington, D.C., as its classroom. You'll spend time on Capitol Hill and in the White House, visit embassies, attend seminars, tour the city, take study tours of monuments and museums, go to the theater, and lodge in a comfortable hotel. Included in the modest cost are in-town transportation, activities and excursions, lodging for six nights, a banquet, a night at the theater, and all meals, some at the popular Washington restaurants.

For information: Close Up Foundation, 44 Canal Center Plaza, Alexandria, VA 22314; 800-363-4762 or 703-706-3668.

THE COLLEGE AT 60

At Fordham University's The College at 60 where, despite its name, you're welcome at a mere 50, you get a discount on courses in liberal arts at Fordham's Lincoln Center Campus. You pay half the regular university tuition to take the courses for credit, and only half of that to audit. The 13-week courses are taught by university faculty. Included are a lecture series and the use of all college facilities. After taking four courses, students receive a certificate and are encouraged to enter the regular Fordham University program for a degree.

For information: The College at 60, Fordham University at Lincoln Center, 113 W. 60th St., Room 804, New York, NY 10023; 212-636-6372.

COLLEGE FOR SENIORS

A membership program for those 55 or older, the College for Seniors is a component of the Center for Creative Retirement at the University of North Carolina at Asheville. Here the courses, most of them taught by peer seniors, range from Chaucer to computers, foreign affairs to opera, and chemistry to tap dancing. Annual membership is $70, plus a per-course fee of $20 or $40, depending on the number of weeks involved. Added benefits include social events, travel programs, wellness clinics, exploration weekends, library privileges, parking decals, and access to the fitness center.

For information: College for Seniors, 104 Carmichael Hall, CPO #1660, UNCA, 1 University Heights, Asheville, NC 28804; 704-251-6384.

ELDERFOLK

Each of Elderfolk's two- to five-week courses in Nepal, India, Tibet, Bhutan, China, and Pakistan focuses on Himalayan culture, history, natural history, religion, native cuisine, and arts and crafts. Exclusively for adventurers over the age of 55, they are offered by the Folkways Institute, a small international school without walls "whose projects are designed to permit cross-cultural understanding," which plans study courses for students and professors.

Some of the courses, combining education and exotic travel, are cultural treks on which you'll be put up at night in roomy tents or lodges. Others are residential or overland trips where you lodge in small hotels or guest houses, such as the Ancient Silk Road trip from Xian to Lahore.

No expertise or training is required, but some stamina definitely is.

For information: Elderfolk, Folkways Institute, 14600 SE Aldridge Rd., Portland, OR 97236-6518; 800-225-4666 or 503-658-6600.

ELDERHOSTEL

The wildly popular educational travel program for mature people, Elderhostel offers some of the world's best bargains and learning experiences. Inexpensive and infinitely varied, its short-term, non-credit college-level programs in the liberal arts and sciences number in the thousands. Courses are hosted by an international network of about 1,800 educational and cultural institutions throughout the U.S., Canada, and over 70 foreign countries. The only requirement for participation is that you must be 55 or over. An accompanying spouse or adult companion may be younger.

Most Elderhostel programs in the U.S. and Canada last five or six nights, while the all-inclusive overseas programs last one to four weeks, with hostelers spending a week at each of one or more locations.

Participants take up to three noncredit courses while living at the host site in a variety of simple but comfortable accommodations ranging from college dormitories to conference centers or nearby hotels or motels. The food is not elaborate, but it is nourishing. Extracurricular activities are usually included. No previous educational background is required and there are no exams, grades, or homework.

The course offerings are myriad, all of them listed in voluminous seasonal catalogs. You may also view them twenty-four hours a day, seven days a week, on the Internet at www.elderhostel.org, where you may search by subject, date, or location.

HOSTELSHIPS

Elderhostel offers a limited number of full or partial scholarships, to be used only in the U.S., for people who find the tuition costs of the programs beyond their means. Funds to cover travel costs are not included and eligibility is determined upon completion of an application that includes a confidential questionnaire. Scholarship programs in Alaska and Hawaii are available only to residents of these states.
For information: Write to Elderhostel, 75 Federal St., Boston MA 02110. Attention: Hostelships.

Costs are astonishingly low, with the typical domestic program costing about $350, which includes everything except transportion to the site. Foreign trips, obviously more expensive, include airfare. For all of the programs, you may register by telephone or by interactive registration system on-line through the website. You may pay by credit card.

Many of the programs include sports and other outdoor adventures such as canoeing, skiing, biking, rafting, walking (see Chapter 13). The Homestay Program (see Chapter 11) lets you live with a foreign family for a week as part of your two-week program. The Service Programs (see Chapter 18) connect you to a wide variety of volunteer organizations providing significant services all over the world. Intergenerational programs for members and their adult children or grandchildren are also an option.

For information: Elderhostel, 75 Federal St., Boston, MA 02110; 877-426-8056 (toll-free) or 617-426-7788; website: www.elderhostel.org. In Canada: Elderhostel Canada, 5 Cataraqui St., Kingston, ON K7K 1Z7; 613-530-2222.

ELDERTREKS

The exotic adventures planned by ElderTreks to places such as China, Nepal, Tibet, Thailand, Vietnam, and Borneo qualify as travel/study trips because they immerse you in the cultures you visit. See Chapter 5 for more.

For information: ElderTreks, 597 Markham St., Toronto, ON M6G 2L7; 800-741-7956 or 416-588-5000.

GOLDEN ID STUDENT PROGRAM

You can get an education for free when you join the University of Maryland's Golden ID Student Program. State residents who are over 60 and employed no more than 20 hours a week may take up to three three-credit regular undergraduate or graduate courses per semester—and pay nothing for the privilege. The only charge is a registration fee and the only hitch is that your acceptance into the program is contingent on space availability in the courses you have chosen.

For information: Golden ID Program, University of Maryland, Mitchell Building, Room 1101, College Park, MD; 301-314-8219. At the University College Campus, 301-985-7930.

INTERHOSTEL

Interhostel specializes in overseas learning vacations all over the world, now including the U.S., for groups of adults over the age of 50 and travelmates over 40. Sponsored by the University of New Hampshire Division of Continuing Education, it offers several weeklong travel programs in the U.S. and more than 75 two-week adventures in other countries. Each program combines lectures and presentations with field trips, sight-seeing, museum visits, and special cultural and social activities.

On the foreign trips, you will live in clean and comfortable—although not necessarily elegant—accommodations, eat the local food, and learn about the land you're in. The moderate cost includes airfare, room, meals, tuition, ground transportation, and all activities. Each program is co-hosted by an overseas university that lends its faculty and provides other local experts. Good physical shape is a requisite for participation because you will be expected to climb stairs, tote your own baggage, and walk comfortably at a moderate pace for at least a mile at a time. See Chapter 13 for Interhostel's walking trips abroad.

Interhostel-USA programs this year take place in the New Hampshire area, cost remarkably little, include all meals, accommodations, and activities, and are led by UNH faculty and representatives.

For information: Interhostel, 6 Garrison Ave., Durham, NH 03824; 800-733-9753 or 603-862-1147.

NATIONAL ACADEMY OF OLDER CANADIANS

Based in Vancouver, the NAOC's mission is to involve older Canadians in lifelong learning and to work in partnership with other nonprofit organizations to develop programs to promote its membership's contribution to society. These programs currently include computer classes, periodic workshops, and discussion groups on issues of special interest. Annual membership fee is $20.

For information: National Academy of Older Canadians, 411 Dunsmuir St., Vancouver, BC V6B 1X4; 604-681-3767.

OASIS

OASIS (Older Adult Service and Information System) is a nonprofit organization sponsored by the May Department Stores Company in collaboration with local hospitals, medical centers, government agencies, and other participants in about 44 locations in 26 cities across the nation. Its purpose is to enrich the lives of people over 55 by providing educational and wellness programs and volunteer opportunities to its members. At its centers, OASIS offers classes ranging from French conversation and the visual arts to dance, bridge, creative writing, history, exercise, classical music, points of law, and prevention of osteoporosis. Also featured are special events such as concerts, plays, and museum exhibits; lectures; and even trips and cruises. If you live in an OASIS city, sign up—this is a good deal. Membership is free.

For information: The OASIS Institute, 7710 Carondelet Ave., Ste. 125, St. Louis, MO 63105; 314-862-2933.

PLUS PROGRAM, NYU

All students over 65 who register for at least one regular course for which they pay half tuition in the School of Continuing Education and Professional Studies at New York University are eligible to become members of PLUS, a Program of Lifelong Learning for University Seniors, for an additional fee of $75 per semester. Membership includes a choice of two specially designed, five-session mini-courses on a broad range of subjects. Topics for the courses, scheduled on Monday, Tuesday, and Thursday afternoons, have recently included Great Decisions in Foreign Policy, Russian Cinema, and the Creative World of Leonard Bernstein. PLUS members may also attend five weekly luncheon/discussion lectures with prominent speakers.

For information: PLUS, NYU School of Continuing Education, 11 W. 42nd St., New York, NY 10036; 212-790-1352 or 212-998-7130.

SAGA HOLIDAYS

Saga Holidays, marketing travel only for people over 50, offers travel/study programs as well as myriad escorted tours and cruises. One is its own series of Smithsonian Odyssey

Tours and another is the Road Scholar program, with itineraries that feature educational themes. The programs include expert lecturers, selected literature, and predeparture educational materials. See Chapter 5 for more.

For information: Saga Holidays, 222 Berkeley St., Boston, MA 02116; 800-343-0273; Smithsonian Odyssey Tours: 800-258-5885. Road Scholar program: 800-621-2151.

SEMESTER AT SEA

A 100-day educational voyage around the world, Semester at Sea, academically sponsored by the University of Pittsburgh and administered by the Institute for Shipboard Education, takes over 600 college students and 50 to 60 "senior scholars" on a unique learning experience designed to advance the exchange of understanding and knowledge between cultures. The S.S. *Universe Explorer*, a former passenger ship refitted as a floating campus, circumnavigates the earth twice a year, visiting countries that have included Japan, China, India, Malaysia, Kenya, Brazil, Venezuela, Egypt, Israel, South Africa, Greece, Turkey, Vietnam, and Morocco.

While the college students earn credit hours toward an undergraduate degree, the older participants may audit classes or enroll for full credit, choosing from among 60 courses taught by faculty from various universities. Onboard courses range from anthropology and biological sciences to economics, fine arts, philosophy, political science, and religion. Lengthy stays in each port of call give students a chance to experience the peoples and cultures firsthand.

Amenities include an adult coordinator, entertainment, buffet-style meals, lectures, discussion groups, guest scholars with expertise in local cultures, films, art shows, sports, and more.

For information: Semester at Sea, 811 William Pitt Union, University of Pittsburgh, Pittsburgh, PA 15260; 800-854-0195 or 412-648-7490.

SENIOR SUMMER SCHOOL

In this program, you can spend two to ten weeks taking classes on your choice of six college campuses in "vacation" locations: San Diego State University, University of Wisconsin, University of California at Santa Barbara, West Virginia University at Morgantown, University of Judaism in Los Angeles, and Mount Allison University in New Brunswick, Canada. The courses are college level but there are no grades, compulsory papers, or mandatory attendance. Accommodations and meals are in university student housing. Sight-seeing trips, excursions, classes, weekly housekeeping, and social activities are all part of the deal. While most students are in their mid-60s, people of any age are welcome to enroll. There are no previous educational requirements.

For information: Senior Summer School, PO Box 4424, Deerfield Beach, FL 33442; 800-847-2466.

SENIOR VENTURES IN OREGON

Southern Oregon University in Ashland offers inexpensive one-week educational theater programs for people at least 50 years of age (and companions who may be younger). The summer programs coincide with the university's famous annual Oregon Shakespeare Festival. Classes are taught by actors, backstage professionals, and Shakespearean scholars. You stay on campus and eat your meals there. Added bonus: theater tickets to current productions.

An alternative residential program combining theater programs with intermediate-level bridge classes are another option for people over 50. A few travel adventures, such as a 10-day tour of the Texas hill country or a Canadian theater expedition, are also offered.

For information: Senior Ventures, Southern Oregon University, 1250 Siskiyou Blvd., Ashland, OR 97520; 800-257-0577 or 541-552-6285.

SENIOR VENTURES IN WASHINGTON

Senior Ventures at Central Washington University in Ellensburg, Washington, is a summer residential program for older adults that offers over 50 courses—with no tests, papers, or grades—taught by university faculty. Students, who may sign up for two-week sessions and take up to six classes a day, are housed in residence-hall suites with private bathrooms and eat in their own cafeteria-style dining hall. Courses range from personal computers and the Internet to baroque art, Chinese customs, modern art, music, tennis, golf, jewelry-making, and psychology. Excursions and weekend field trips are included, as are evening activities.

For information: Senior Ventures, CWU, 400 E. 8th Ave., Ellensburg, WA 98926; 800-752-4380 or 509-963-1526.

TRAVELEARN

The upscale learning vacations by TraveLearn take small groups of adults all over the world, putting you up in first-class or deluxe accommodations and providing faculty escorts chosen from a network of more than 300 cooperating universities and colleges, as well as local lecturers, in each place you visit. You'll learn through on-site lectures, seminars, meals with local families, visits to homes and workplaces, and field trips. Destinations include Ireland, Egypt, Kenya, Indonesia, China, Morocco, Greece, Israel, Italy, Turkey, South Africa, Costa Rica, Peru, and more. If you are traveling alone and wish to share a room with another single traveler, you are guaranteed the double rate

LEARNING COMPUTER TECHNOLOGY

SeniorNet is a national nonprofit organization dedicated to building a community of computer-literate older adults, providing them with information and instruction about computer technologies. It sponsors 140 community-based SeniorNet Learning Centers nationwide where members may take classes and use the facilities. Independent members participate through the organization's electronic community, SeniorNet Online.

Membership costs $35 ($40 for couples) for the first year and $25 (or $30) after that. Among its benefits are a quarterly newsletter, discounts on computer-related books, software and hardware, and invitations to national conferences and regional meetings.

SeniorNet maintains two websites, one on the Internet and the other on AOL. Internet: www.seniornet.org. AOL: seniornet.

For information: SeniorNet, 121 Second St., San Francisco, CA 94105; 800-747-6848 or 415-352-1210; E-mail: senior net@aol.com.

if you register 90 days in advance, even if a roommate is not found for you.

For information: TraveLearn, PO Box 315, Lakeville, PA 18438; 800-235-9114 or 717-226-9114.

UNIVERSITY VACATIONS

Summer scholars may attend a range of 6- to 12-day study programs at such prestigious institutions as the Sorbonne in Paris, the University of Bologna in Italy, the University of Leiden in the Netherlands, Harvard University in the U.S., and Oxford University in England. In-depth classroom lectures by university faculty are augmented by field trips, walking tours, excursions, and notable meals. Students live on campus or in nearby hotels and eat in fine restaurants. The programs are open to all ages but are largely attended by older students.

For information: University Vacations, 3660 Bougainvillea Rd., Coconut Grove, FL 33133; 800-792-0100 or 305-567-2904.

INSTITUTES FOR LEARNING IN RETIREMENT

Another way to get an education with a group of contemporaries is to join an ILR. Sponsored by almost 250 colleges and universities around the country, ILRs provide non-credit, college-level courses for older adults, most of them retirees, who can attend daytime classes at schools close to home. Students frequently help design the curriculum and often lead some of the classes. Enrollment policies and age requirements at ILRs vary, but in most cases you don't have to worry about exams, term papers, or grades. You pay a modest annual membership fee and, at some institutions, you may take regular undergraduate courses too if you wish.

For a directory of current Institutes for Learning in Retirement, and/or information about starting a new program, contact the Elderhostel Institute Network, an association of independent ILRs.

For information: Elderhostel Institute Network, 75 Federal St., Boston, MA 02110; 617-422-0784.

17

Shopping Breaks, Taxes, Insurance, and Other Practical Matters

I n this chapter you won't find suggestions for interesting vacation possibilities, or unusual places to explore. Instead, you'll get useful information about benefits and services that could be coming to you simply because you are now sufficiently mature to take advantage of them.

SAVE MONEY IN THE STORES

All over the U.S. and Canada and even other parts of the world, retail stores now offer discounts to seniors because they realize that mature people tend to be cautious consumers who know the value of a dollar, are extremely fond of bargains, and have the potential of becoming loyal customers. In fact, the older population has now started to expect reduced prices when they shop.

Stores vary on the age at which you may receive their special offers, but most start you off at 60. Some give you 10 or 15 percent off every day, while others reserve one day a week for their senior discounts. Sometimes, however, instead of discounts, they advertise senior specials. Sears and Montgomery Ward, on the other hand, have clubs to join that entitle you to special discounts and other services.

MONTGOMERY WARD Y.E.S. CLUB

Montgomery Ward's Y.E.S. (Years of Extra Savings) Discount Club saves you money in many ways when you've reached the age of 55. As a member, you receive a membership card and a bimonthly magazine called *Vantage*. The membership fee is currently $3.49 per month or $34.99 a year for you and your spouse. With the membership card in hand, you will get 10 percent off any merchandise, sale or nonsale, in all Montgomery Ward stores every Tuesday. On Tuesdays, Wednesdays, and Thursdays, you're entitled to 10 percent off any auto labor charges. There are other benefits as well, such as pharmacy-by-mail and auto-pricing services.

What's more, the Y.E.S. Club Travel Service plans your travel, makes reservations, and gives you discounted prices plus cash rebates of 10 percent off all lodging and car rentals, and 5 percent on tours, cruises, rail passes, and airline tickets.

For information: Montgomery Ward Y.E.S. Discount Club, 200 N. Martingale Rd., Schaumburg, IL 60173; 800-421-5396.

SEARS MATURE OUTLOOK

Mature Outlook, a membership program for Sears card-holders age 45 and over, now comes in two varieties: the original Mature Outlook Program and Mature Outlook Plus. Both programs provide a variety of benefits and savings, including money coupons to be used for the store's products and services. Coupons are included in the club's magazine and in the annual membership kit and may be used in all Sears stores in the country. See Chapter 19 for more about Mature Outlook and what it offers its members.

For information: Mature Outlook, PO Box 9390, Des Moines, IA 50306. Mature Outlook Program: 800-336-6330. Mature Outlook Plus: 800-688-5665.

FEDERAL INCOME TAXES

The tax laws no longer provide an extra exemption for people over the age of 65. Instead, they give you a larger standard deduction than younger people are entitled to, according to Julian Block, a Larchmont, New York, tax attorney and author of a popular guide to saving on income taxes, *Julian Block's Tax Avoidance Secrets.*

The standard deductions for everyone under 65 for 1999 returns are $7,200 for married couples filing jointly; $3,600 each for married people filing separately; $4,300 for single people; and $6,350 for heads of households. These standard deductions change every year to reflect inflation, so be sure to check them out for each year's return.

If one spouse of a couple filing jointly is over 65, the standard deduction is increased for 1999 returns (by $850) to $8,050. If both members of a married couple are over 65, it is increased (by $850 twice) to $8,900.

For a married person over 65 filing separately, the deduction increases (by $850) to $4,450. A single person over 65 may deduct $5,350 ($1,050 more than those who are younger) and a head of household over 65 gets a standard deduction in 1999 of $7,400 ($1,050 more than an under-65).

None of these figures apply, of course, if you itemize your deductions. Remember that at age 65 you needn't file returns at all when your reportable income is below the amount required for filing.

By the way, the Internal Revenue Service issues a free booklet, *Tax Information for Older Americans* (Publication No. 554), which you can get at your local IRS office or by calling 800-TAX-FORM. You may also want to ask for its free *Guide to Free Tax Services* (Publication No. 910), which provides a list of IRS booklets on federal taxes and explains what each one covers. Request large-print tax forms if you need them.

HOW TO GET HELP
WITH YOUR TAX RETURN

Assistance in preparing your tax returns is available free from both the Internal Revenue Service and AARP. The IRS offers Tax Counseling for the Elderly (TCE) for people over 60 and Voluntary Income Tax Assistants (VITA) for younger people who need help. Trained volunteers provide information and will prepare returns at thousands of sites throughout the country from February 2 to April 15. Watch your local newspaper for a list of sites in your area or call 800-TAX-1040 and press 0.

Or you may enlist the help of AARP's Tax-Aide Service at more than 10,000 sites nationwide where, in the 10-week period before April 15, volunteers help low- and moderate-income members of AARP to prepare their tax returns. Volunteers will even go to your home, when necessary, if you are physically unable to get to a site. To find the site nearest you, call 888-AARP-NOW (800-227-7669). Or call your regional or state AARP offices. Have your membership number and zip code handy and also your calendar, as an appointment is required.

SAVE ON AUTO AND HOMEOWNER'S INSURANCE

Among the nice surprises waiting for you on your 50th or 55th birthday is the possibility of paying less for your automobile and homeowner's insurance because of lower claims costs. So try to take advantage of your age when you shop for a new policy or renew an existing one.

Mature drivers get breaks because, as a group, they tend to be cautious drivers, much more careful than the younger crowd, having shed their bad habits such as speeding and reckless driving. And, although older drivers total more accidents per mile, they drive fewer miles, usually don't use their cars for daily commuting, and tend to stay off the roads at night and in bad weather. If they are retired, they don't use their cars every day in rush-hour traffic. Therefore, statistically, they have fewer accidents per driver than other risk categories do, at least until they are over the age of 75.

In addition, you may get a discount—usually 10 percent—on some of your automobile coverage in most states when you successfully complete a state-approved defensive-driving course. Among the programs is AARP's 55 Alive/Mature Driving, an eight-hour classroom refresher that specifically addresses the needs of older drivers with physical and perceptual changes that affect their driving. Open to both AARP members and nonmembers at a current cost of $8 per person, and taught by volunteers, the course is offered locally all over the country. Defensive-driving courses are also offered by other groups, including local high schools and the AAA.

Homeowners over a certain age are also considered better risks for insurance claims than younger people because they spend more time at home where they can keep an eye on things and take care of their property. So some companies offer older people reductions on premiums too.

Although discounts are wonderful and we all love to get them, they aren't everything. Always shop the bottom line when you buy insurance. In other words, know what you are getting for what you are paying. Rates for the same coverage can differ by hundreds of dollars, so you must be a comparison shopper to get the best deal. If one company charges higher premiums for comparable coverage and then gives you a discount, you have not profited.

Insurance regulations differ from state to state, but here are some of the offerings made in some states to older drivers and homeowners by some major insurance companies.

Always ask for the discounts that may be coming to you because agents don't always volunteer this information. In addition to your age-related discount, ask about others. Some insurers offer discounts for insuring more than one car on the same policy, clean driving records, antitheft devices, low mileage, more than one policy with the same company, and longtime coverage. And watch out for policies that bump up your costs again when you turn 70.

HOW TO SAVE YOUR LIFE

If you get sick or have an accident away from home, a non-profit foundation called **MedicAlert** may save your health or even your life. For an initial fee of $35 and $15 a year thereafter, you receive a stainless-steel bracelet or neck chain engraved with your personal identification number, a 24-hour-a-day toll-free telephone number, and a brief description of your medical condition. Information about your treatment is kept on file and is available by telephone to you or medical personnel who may need it in an emergency. Included are names and telephone numbers of your physicians and those to notify if necessary. As a backup, you get a wallet card with the same information printed on it.

For information: MedicAlert Foundation, PO Box 1009, Turlock, CA 95381; 800-344-3226.

ALLSTATE

Allstate gives a discount of 10 percent off the premiums across the board—liability, comprehensive, and collision coverage—on automobile insurance in almost every state for those who are 55 and retired and an additional 5 or 10 percent off for taking an approved defensive-driving course.

As for property coverage, Allstate offers 10 percent off the premiums in most states to homeowners at age 55, 10 percent to renters, and 5 percent to condominium owners who are retired.

AMERICAN FAMILY

If you are between the ages of 50 and 69, American Family gives you 10 percent off on almost all auto coverages. Preferred customers—those with good driving records—who buy both auto and homeowner insurance from this company get another discount of about 10 percent. Not only that, but taking a defensive-driving course nets you an additional 5 to 10 percent discount in some states.

CHUBB GROUP

If you are age 50 through 64, Chubb will give you a 20 percent credit on automobile coverage; from age 65 through 79, you get a 15 percent credit. After that, you revert to the base rate you paid when you were younger. Inquire about a defensive-driving discount and a rate reduction for pleasure driving only.

COLONIAL PENN

Homeowners age 55 or more who work less than 24 hours a week get a credit of 10 to 30 percent on policies covering their principal residences. Drivers age 55 and at least semiretired are offered 5 to 10 percent off liability coverage and about 15 percent off coverage for physical damage to their vehicles. If you are now driving fewer miles than you once did, check to see if you are entitled to a change in mileage classification which can also lower your premium discount for passing a driving course.

FARMERS

Policyholders over the age of 50 or 55 are offered discounts of 7 to 15 percent on automobile coverage in most states where Farmers Insurance is sold if they complete an approved defensive-driving course. A homeowner's credit starts at age 50 and ranges from 2 to 10 percent, depending on your age and the state in which you reside.

GEICO

As a general rule, GEICO applies a lower rate on all automobile coverages for good drivers between the ages of 50 and 74, retired or not, on the cars they principally operate that are not used for business. A certificate from an approved driving course takes off another 10 percent. In addition, a Prime Time contract, available in many states, is offered to households in which the principal operator is over 50, no one on the policy is under 25, and drivers have had no accidents or driving convictions within the last three years. Once issued, this policy guarantees to continue to renew your coverage henceforth, regardless of age, accidents, or driving convictions.

THE HARTFORD

This company underwrites the auto and homeowners insurance designed for AARP members, all of whom are over 50. It gives you discounts for clean driving records, combined policies, safety devices, and completion of an accredited driving course. It also guarantees that you cannot be refused renewal if you fulfill a few requirements such as paying your premiums on time.

HOW TO FIND LOCAL ELDER SERVICES

For information about housing, home health services, adult day care centers, legal assistance, or other kinds of services for older people, call the Eldercare Locator at 800-677-1116. This nationwide governmental resource for elderly people or their caregivers will help you find an appropriate agency or program in your area. Call between 9 A.M. and 8 P.M. (Eastern Time) Monday through Friday and explain the problem. Be sure you know the name, address, and zip code of the person needing help.

As a homeowner, you'll get a discount of up to 10 percent if you and your spouse are retired or work less than 24 hours a week.

NATIONWIDE

This company reduces premiums by 5 percent on all coverage from ages 50 to 54 in most states. From 55 to 69, you'll get a 10 percent discount; from 70 on, you get only a 5 percent reduction once more. Take a defensive-driving course and almost everywhere you'll be entitled to an additional 5 to 15 percent off.

PROGRESSIVE

This large insurance company offers a free 24-hour automobile insurance rate comparison service to help you decide on the best rate for you, discounts or not. If you dial 800-AUTO-PRO, you will get rate comparisons for up to four different major insurance companies, including Progressive, in your state.

PRUDENTIAL

Prudential gives drivers ages 50 through 54 a discount of about 10 percent in most states, 15 percent for ages 55 through 64, 10 percent for ages 65 through 74. You'll get an additional discount of 5 to 10 percent when you complete a defensive-driving course.

On homeowner insurance, there's a 5 percent Mature Homeowner Credit if one owner on the policy is 55 or more.

STATE FARM

In most states, State Farm lowers the rates about 10 percent for drivers over 50 and does not raise them again at 70 or 75, as many other companies do. Get an additional break by taking a driving course.

TRAVELERS

With this insurance company (now merged with Aetna's property and casualty division), the discount you get across the board on automobile coverage varies according to your age. From ages 50 through 64, the discount amounts to 10 to 15 percent depending on the state in which you live. From 65 through 74, it's 15 to 20 percent; and over 75, 5 to 10 percent. Completing a defensive-driving course will add another 5 percent discount in some states for those over 55. The vehicle must be used essentially for pleasure and no driver may be under 25 years of age.

On homeowner insurance, you will get 10 to 20 percent reductions on premiums, depending on the state, when you are 50 or more.

BANKING

Many banks offer special incentives and services to their mature customers, including free checks; elimination of monthly service charges; no-fee traveler's checks, cashier's checks, and money orders; and free safe-deposit boxes. All banks and state regulations are different so you must do some comparison shopping to be sure you are receiving the best deal available in your community.

LEGAL ASSISTANCE

Call upon your local area senior agency, which is required by law to provide some legal assistance to older citizens. Yours may help you untangle some puzzling legal problems or, at least, tell you what services are available to you. Or contact your local bar association for information about referrals or pro bono programs; or the National Academy of Elder Law Attorneys (520-881-4005 or www.naela.org), which sells directories that list its members by region.

In the majority of states and the District of Columbia, the AARP Legal Services Network now provides AARP members, via their local Yellow Pages, with a list of pre-screened attorneys who have agreed to rigorous guidelines and discounted fees for services. Check your Yellow Pages under the "Attorneys," "Lawyers," or "Associations" sections to find participating attorneys in your area.

18

Volunteer for Great Experiences

If, perhaps for the first time in your life, you have time, expertise, talent, and energy to spare, consider volunteering your services to organizations that could use your help. There is plenty of significant work waiting for you and more and more older Americans are volunteering as a way of finding fulfillment both before and after retirement. If you are looking for a good match between your abilities and a program that needs them, take a look at the programs described here, all of them specifically seeking the experience and enthusiasm of mature adults.

But, first, keep in mind:

When you file your federal income tax, you may be allowed to deduct unreimbursed expenses incurred while volunteering your services to a charitable organization. You may be able to deduct program fees and reasonable costs for transportation, parking, tolls, meals, lodging, and uniforms. You may not be able to take off all of your travel expenses, meals, and lodging, however, when you spend a significant amount of personal or vacation time before, during, or after a service program, or if you get benefit from your service, such as academic credit.

AARP VOLUNTEER TALENT BANK

VTB is a nationwide computerized volunteer-reference service that matches the interests and skills of AARP members who wish to volunteer their services with programs, projects, and organizations that can use their help in their own neighborhoods. The volunteer programs range from AARP community programs, such as Tax Aide, 55 Alive/Mature Driving, and Health Advocacy, to well-known national organizations such as the American Red Cross, Habitat for Humanity, Recording for the Blind, March of Dimes, and the U.S. National Fish and Wildlife Service.

For information: Volunteer Talent Bank, 601 E St. NW, Washington, DC 20049; 202-434-3219.

ELDERHOSTEL SERVICE PROGRAMS

Elderhostel Service Programs tap the experience and expertise of older adults (55 or over) in short-term volunteer projects in the U.S., Canada, and throughout the world. Teams of hostelers are paired with nonprofit organizations for a wide variety of service activities, from historical preservation to teaching English to natural-resources conservation, working with children with special needs, archaeological research, and even helping to build affordable housing. No special skills or experience are required. A 55-plus volunteer may be accompanied by an adult who is younger.

Currently more than 83 institutions and organizations—far too many to list here—are collaborating with Elderhostel to put mature Americans, retired or not, to work for one to three weeks per session in the U.S. or in other countries of the world. These include such diverse groups as Habitat for Humanity, Oceanic Society Expeditions, the U.S. Forest Service, Global Volunteers, Cross-Cultural Solutions, Appalachian Mountain Club, Hole in the Woods Ranch, the Center for Bioacoustics, the Museum of Science and Industry in Chicago, Grand Canyon National Park, and many more.

The fee you must pay to participate varies with each program and includes full room and board, equipment, social and cultural events, and, in most cases, airfare.

For information: Elderhostel, 75 Federal St., Boston, MA 02110; 877-426-8056 or 617-426-7788. In Canada: Elderhostel Canada, 5 Cataraqui St., Kingston, ON K7K 1Z7; 613-530-2222.

FAMILY FRIENDS

A national program sponsored by the National Council on Aging, Family Friends recruits volunteers over the age of 55 to work with children with disabilities, chronic illnesses, or other problems in many locations around the country. The volunteers act as caring grandparents, helping the families in whatever ways they can, mostly dealing with children at home but occasionally in hospitals. They are asked to serve at least four hours a week and to commit themselves to the program for at least a year. Volunteers are reimbursed for expenses incurred.

The local projects are funded by the federal government, corporations, foundations, and local, county, city, or state governments.

For information: Family Friends Resource Center, 409 Third St. SW, Washington, DC 20024; 202-479-6675.

HOW TO HELP THE ENVIRONMENT

Environmental Alliance for Senior Involvement (EASI) is designed to tap the talents, knowledge, experience, and enthusiasm of older people interested in the environment. Together with local and national senior and environmental organizations such as AARP, RSVP, the EPA, the National Council on Aging, World Wildlife Fund, and National Wildlife Federation, volunteers work to preserve and restore the environment in their own communities. Current projects include pollution control, water source protection, solar energy installations, brown fields, and radon identification.
For information: EASI, 8733 Old Dumfries Rd., Catlett, VA 20119; 540-788-3274.

FOSTER GRANDPARENTS

Foster Grandparents devote their volunteer service to children with special or exceptional needs. They provide emotional support to victims of abuse and neglect, mentor troubled teenagers and young mothers, care for premature infants and children with physical disabilities and severe illnesses, and tutor children who lag behind in reading. Volunteers must be 60 or older, meet certain income-eligibility guidelines, and serve 20 hours a week, usually 4 hours a day Monday through Friday, in facilities in their own neighborhoods.

For this, they receive—in addition to the immense satisfaction—modest tax-free stipends to offset their costs, some meals during service, reimbursement for transportation, an annual physical examination, and accident and liability insurance while on duty.

For information: Contact your local Foster Grandparents program, or the Corporation for National Service, 1201 New York Ave. NW, Washington, DC 20525; 800-424-8867.

INTERNATIONAL EXECUTIVE SERVICE CORPS

IESC, organized and directed by U.S. business executives, is a nonprofit organization that recruits retired, highly skilled executives and technical advisors to assist businesses in the developing nations. It is funded by the U.S. Agency for International Development (AID), overseas clients and foreign governments, and many American corporations.

After being briefed on the country and the client, volunteer executives travel overseas—with their spouses, if they wish—for projects that generally last two to three months. IESC pays for the couple's travel expenses and provides a per diem allowance.

For information: International Executive Service Corps, 333 Ludlow St., Stamford, CT 06902; 800-243-4372 or 203-967-6000.

NATIONAL EXECUTIVE SERVICE CORPS

This nonprofit organization performs a unique service: it helps other nonprofit organizations solve their problems by providing retired executives with extensive corporate and professional experience to serve as volunteer consultants. Its services are offered in five basic areas—education, health, the arts, social services, and religion—and the assistance covers everything from organizational structure and financial systems to marketing and funding strategy. Volunteers' expenses are covered.

For information: National Executive Service Corps, 120 Wall St., New York, NY 10005; 212-269-1234.

NATIONAL PARK SERVICE

If you love the outdoors and have the time, volunteer to work for the National Park Service as a VIP (Volunteers in Parks). VIPs are not limited to over-50s, but a good portion of them are retired people with time, expertise, talent, and interest in forests and wilderness. You may work a few hours a week or a month, seasonally or full-time, and may or may not—depending on the park—wear a uniform or get reimbursed for out-of-pocket expenses. The job possibilities range from working at an information desk to serving as a guide, maintaining trails, driving a shuttle bus, painting fences, designing computer programs, patrolling trails, making wildlife counts, writing visitor brochures, and preparing park events.

For information: Contact the VIP coordinator at the national park where you would like to volunteer and request an application. Or, write to Volunteer Coordinator, National

Park Service, 18th and C Sts. NW, Ste. 3045, Washington, DC 20240.

NATIONAL TRUST WORKING HOLIDAYS

Britain's National Trust runs hundreds of "working holidays" in England, Wales, and Northern Ireland, inviting volunteers to exchange work for an interesting and low-cost holiday. The National Trust, which oversees Britain's historic and environmental treasures, organizes small groups of people to lend a hand for one-week sessions in such tasks as restoring historic buildings, clearing ponds, or maintaining footpaths. Most programs accept anybody over the age of 18, but several—the Oak Plus Projects—are reserved for enthusiasts between 50 and 70 who are willing to tackle outdoor work.

Lodging is in dormitory-style base camps and the work is paced to allow ample time to relax, take in the local attractions, or go for a stroll.

For information: The National Trust, PO Box 84, Cirencester, Glos, GL7 1ZP, England.

PEACE CORPS

It may surprise you to learn that the Peace Corps is a viable choice for idealists of any age. Eighty is the upper age limit for acceptance into the Peace Corps, and since its beginning in 1961 thousands of Senior Volunteers have brought their talents and experience to almost 100 countries all over the world. To become a Senior Volunteer, you must be a U.S. citizen and meet basic legal and medical criteria. Some assignments require a college or technical-school degree or an experience equivalent. Married couples are eligible and will be assigned together. Service is typically for two years.

What you get in return is the chance to travel, an unforgettable living experience in a foreign land, basic expenses, and housing, plus technical, language, and cultural training. You'll also have a chance to use your expertise constructively in fields such as agriculture, engineering, math/science, home economics, education, skilled trades, forestry and fisheries, and community development.

For information: Peace Corps, 1990 K St. NW, Washington, DC 20526; 800-424-8580.

RSVP (RETIRED AND SENIOR VOLUNTEER PROGRAM)

RSVP matches the interests and skills of men and women over the age of 55 with volunteer opportunities in their own communities. Volunteers, who may serve anywhere from a few to over 40 hours a week, may choose to tutor children, help build houses, provide model parenting skills to teen parents, plan community gardens, deliver meals, offer disaster relief to victims of disasters, work in day-care centers, or do whatever their own communities need. They are not paid but they do receive supplemental insurance while on duty, a preservice orientation, and on-the-job training from the agency or organization where they are placed.

For information: Contact your local or regional RSVP office or Corporation for National Service, 1201 New York Ave. NW, Washington, DC 20525; 800-424-8867.

SENIOR ENVIRONMENTAL EMPLOYMENT PROGRAM (SEE)

The SEE Program, administered by the Environmental Protection Agency (EPA), establishes grants to private nonprofit organizations to recruit, hire, and pay experienced people over the age of 55 to help fight environmental problems. The recruits, who work part-time or full-time in EPA offices or in the field, are paid by the hour in jobs ranging from secretarial and clerical work to highly specialized technical and scientific positions. All are designed to assist the agency in protecting and/or cleaning up the environment.

For information: Contact your regional EPA office or SEE Program, EPA, 401 M St. SW, Washington, DC 20460; 202-260-2574.

SENIOR COMPANIONS

Senior Companions help frail older adults, adults with disabilities, and adults with serious or terminal illnesses who need extra assistance to live independently in their own homes or communities. They provide companionship and friendship to isolated seniors, assist them with simple chores, and provide needed transportation. Volunteers must be 60 or older, meet certain income eligibility guidelines, and serve 20 hours a week, usually 4 hours a day Monday through Friday. Although they are not paid, they receive a modest tax-free stipend, reimbursement for transportation, some meals during service, on-duty accident and liability insurance, and an annual physical examination.

For information: Corporation for National Service, 1201 New York Ave. NW, Washington, DC 20525; 800-424-8867.

SERVICE CORPS OF RETIRED EXECUTIVES (SCORE)

SCORE is a volunteer group of working and retired business leaders who donate their time and talents to counsel owners and would-be owners of small businesses who need expert advice. It offers seminars and workshops plus one-on-one counseling, including counseling via its website (www.score.org). A resource partner of the U.S. Small Business Administration, SCORE has a membership of about 12,400 men and women and has almost 389 chapters around the country.

For information: Contact your local U.S. Small Business Administration office or SCORE, 409 Third St. SW, 6th floor, Washington, DC 20024; 800-634-0245 or 202-205-6762.

SERVICE OPPORTUNITIES FOR OLDER PEOPLE (SOOP)

SOOP, sponsored by the Mennonite Board of Missions and other organizations, provides a way for older people of all persuasions to contribute their experience and skills in a variety of locations throughout the U.S. and Canada. You may sign up for a few weeks or up to six months, living at the site and working to help others in need in whatever way you can, from teaching, building, and child care to homemaking, farming, and administering. Once you decide on

FORTY PLUS

Offices in 20 cities throughout the United States comprise this nonprofit cooperative of unemployed executives, managers, and professionals, men and women, who have earned at least $40,000 a year or are 40 years of age or more. Their objective is to help members conduct effective job searches and find new jobs. There is no paid staff. The members do all the work and help pay expenses by paying $500 upon acceptance and then $100 a month thereafter. They must commit themselves to attend weekly meetings and spend at least two days a week working at the club and assisting others in their search for work.

In return, members are helped to examine their career skills and define their goals, counseled on résumé writing and interview skills, helped to plan marketing strategy, and given job leads. They may also use the premises as a base of operations, with phone answering and mail service, computers, and reference library.

Forty Plus exists at this writing in New York City and Buffalo, New York; Oakland, San Diego, San Jose, and Los Angeles (with a branch in Laguna Hills), California; Fort Collins, Colorado Springs, and Lakewood, Colorado; Columbus, Ohio; Dallas and Houston, Texas; Murray, Ogden, and Provo, Utah; Philadelphia, Pennsylvania; Bellevue, Washington; Washington, D.C.; St. Paul, Minnesota; and Honolulu, Hawaii.

For information: Addresses of locations and descriptive materials are available from Forty Plus of New York, 15 Maiden Lane, New York, NY 10038; 212-233-6086.

the kind of work and time commitment you prefer, you make plans with a location coordinator for your assignment and housing. Volunteers usually pay for their own travel, food, and lodging.

For information: Mennonite Board of Missions, PO Box 370, Elkhart, IN 46515; 219-294-7523.

SHEPHERD'S CENTERS OF AMERICA (SCA)

An interfaith, nonprofit organization of older adults who volunteer their skills to help seniors in their communities, SCA has about 90 centers in 26 states. Supported by Catholic, Jewish, and Protestant congregations as well as businesses and foundations, the centers operate many programs designed to enable older people to remain in their own homes as active participants in community life. They also encourage intergenerational interaction. Centers offer such in-home services as Telephone Visitors, Family Friends, Meals on Wheels, Handyhands Service, and Respite Care, all provided mostly by volunteers. Programs at the centers include other services, day trips, classes, and courses as well as support groups and referrals. Membership is open to anyone over the age of 55.

For information: Shepherd's Centers of America, 1 W. Armour, Ste. 201, Kansas City, MO 64111; 800-547-7073.

VOLUNTEER GRANDPARENTS SOCIETY

The objective of this nonprofit organization in Canada is to match volunteer grandparents with families with children between the ages of 3 and 12 who have no accessible grandparents. The volunteers, who are not paid and do not commit to a contract or specific hours, establish a relationship of mutual enjoyment, support, and caring and become part of an extended family. They are also placed in school classrooms, serving as a supportive presence for the children. Applicants are interviewed and carefully screened, and matches are based on compatibility as well as on geographic proximity. The organization, which originated in 1973 in Vancouver, has expanded with the development of programs across Canada in addition to several located in British Columbia.

For information: Volunteer Grandparents, #3, 1734 W. Broadway, Vancouver, BC V6J 1Y1; 604-736-8271.

JOB PROGRAM FOR OLDER WORKERS

Senior Community Service Employment Program (SCSEP), a federally funded program, recruits unemployed low-income men and women over the age of 55, assesses their employment strengths, and hires them for paid jobs in community-service positions. At the same time, the enrollees begin training in new job skills and receive such help as counseling, physical examinations, group meetings, and job fairs while the agency tries to match them with permanent jobs in the private sector. If you qualify and are looking for a paying position, this agency is worth a try.

For information: SCSEP, National Council on the Aging, 409 Third St. SW, Washington, DC 20024; 202-479-1200. Or contact your local, county, or state Office for the Aging.

VOLUNTEERS IN TECHNICAL ASSISTANCE

VITA provides another avenue for helping developing countries. A nonprofit international organization, VITA provides volunteer experts who respond—usually by direct correspondence—to technical inquiries from people in these nations who need assistance in such areas as small-business development, energy applications, agriculture, reforestation, water supply and sanitation, and low-cost housing. Its volunteers also perform other services such as project planning, translations, publications, marketing strategies, evaluations, and technical reports and often become on-site consultants.

There is no minimum age, but you must be retired to serve. If you become a volunteer, you will not be paid, but you will be reimbursed for your travel and living expenses. *For information:* Volunteers in Technical Assistance, 1600 Wilson Blvd., Ste. 710, Arlington, VA 22209; 703-276-1800.

VOLUNTEER PROGRAMS IN ISRAEL
ACTIVE RETIREES IN ISRAEL (ARI)

Sponsored by B'nai B'rith International, ARI is a volunteer work program for people who are at least 50 and in good health. Volunteers pay for the opportunity to live in the resort city of Netanya and work in the mornings for one or two months in hospitals, forests, kibbutzim, schools, and facilities for the elderly and the handicapped. Afternoons are spent learning Hebrew, while the evenings include concerts, discussion groups, and cultural activities. Guided tours of the country are part of the program. Optional trips to Eilat and Petra in Jordan are available as add-ons to your stay.

For information: ARI, B'nai B'rith Center for Jewish Identity, 1640 Rhode Island Ave. NW, Washington, DC 20036; 800-500-6533 or 202-857-6580.

JEWISH NATIONAL FUND

To qualify for the JNF Canadian American Active Retirees in Israel (CA-ARI), a two- to ten-week winter program sponsored by the Jewish National Fund, you must be over 50 and in good physical and mental health. Your time will be spent working five mornings a week, tending the JNF national forests and, in addition, working at a choice of other jobs. Some volunteers choose to contribute their time in schools, hospitals, homes for the aged, army bases, or universities, while others assist local craftspeople. After-noons are devoted to planned activities such as sight-see-ing trips, cultural and social events, and lectures; and evenings to socializing. Included is a tour of the country and time in Jerusalem.

For information: JNF CA-ARI Program, Missions Dept., 42 E. 69th St., New York, NY 10021; 800-223-7787 or 212-879-9305, ext. 284.

VOLUNTEERS FOR ISRAEL

In this volunteer work-and-cultural program for adults 18 and older in Israel, you'll put in eight-hour days for three weeks, sleep in a segregated dormitory, and work in small groups at a reserve or supply military base, doing whatever needs doing most at that moment. You may serve in sup-ply, warehousing, or maintenance of equipment or in social services in hospitals. You'll wear an army uniform with a "Civilian Volunteer" patch. Board, room, and other expenses are free, but you must pay for your own partially subsidized airfare.

For information: Volunteers for Israel, 330 West 42nd St., 16th floor, New York, NY 10036; 212-643-4848.

WINTER AND SPRING IN NETANYA

Hadassah's Winter in Netanya (WIN) and Springtime in Netanya (SPIN) programs combine work, vacation, and study in Israel. For one or two months, participants live in a four-

---

OPERATION ABLE

If you're over 40 and in the market for a job but don't know where to start looking for one, hook up with **Operation ABLE**, a nonprofit organization affiliated with a network of agencies that will help match you with a likely employer. You're in luck if you live in the Chicago area, where there are six regional offices. But there is also a network of independent ABLE-like organizations, modeled after the original, in several other cities, including Boston; Denver; Los Angeles; Lincoln, Neb.; Rockville, Md.; Southfield, Mich.; and St. Albans, Vt.

Operation ABLE tries every which way to get you into the working world. It provides job counseling, on-the-job training, group training activities, and individual career assessment and guidance; teaches job-hunting skills; matches older workers with employers; operates a pool of temporaries; and offers many other services.

For information: Operation ABLE, 180 N. Wabash Ave., Chicago, IL 60601; 312-782-3335.

---

star hotel in a Mediterranean resort town 20 miles north of Tel Aviv. They pay for their privileges by donating their mornings to working in hospitals, schools, community centers, and army bases; teaching English to new immigrants; planting gardens; painting murals; and doing carpentry. Afternoons are devoted to optional conversational Hebrew lessons, sight-seeing, and relaxation, while the evenings are reserved for social and cultural events. The participants, many of them retirees, also spend a week in Jerusalem and go on special excursions to such places as Masada and Safed as well as museums, archaeological sites, and a kibbutz.

For information: Hadassah, 50 West 58th St., New York, NY 10019; 212-303-8133 or your local Hadassah chapter.

19

The Over-50 Organizations and What They Can Do for You

When you consider that there are more people in this country over the age of 55 than there are children in elementary and high schools, you can see why we have powerful potential to influence what goes on around here. As the demographic discovery of the times, a group that controls most of the nation's disposable income, we've become a prime marketing target. And, just like any other large group of people, we've got plenty of needs.

A number of organizations in the United States and Canada have been formed in recent years to act as advocates for the mature population and to provide us with special programs as well as opportunities to spend our money on their products or services. Here is a brief rundown on them and what they have to offer you. You may want to join more than one of them so you can get the best of each.

AARP (AMERICAN ASSOCIATION OF RETIRED PERSONS)

At age 50 you are eligible to join AARP, the extensive non-profit organization that serves as an advocate for the older generation, offers a vast array of services and programs, and sells many kinds of insurance. With more than 32 million members, it is one of the most effective lobbying groups in the country. You do not have to be retired to join. Its newsletter *AARP Bulletin* and magazine *Modern Maturity* go to more homes than any other publications in the U.S. For an annual membership fee of $8 (and that includes a spouse), AARP offers so many benefits that you are likely to stop reading before the end of the list. But here are some of them:

- Group health insurance, life insurance, auto insurance, homeowner's insurance, mobile-home insurance
- Discounts on hotels, motels, auto rentals, and sight-seeing
- A mail-order pharmacy service that delivers prescription and nonprescription drugs
- A motoring plan that includes emergency road and towing services, trip planning, and other benefits
- A national advocacy and lobbying program at all levels of government to develop legislative priorities and represent the interests of older people
- More than 4,000 local chapters with their own activities and volunteer projects
- The Volunteer Talent Bank, which matches you with volunteer opportunities in your community

■ A series of employment planning workshops called AARP Works for older job hunters

■ Special programs in a wide range of areas such as consumer affairs, legal counseling, financial information, housing, health advocacy, voter education, employment planning, independent living, disability initiatives, grandparent information, and public benefits

■ Tax-Aide, a program conducted in cooperation with the IRS that helps lower- and moderate-income members with their income tax returns

■ 55 ALIVE/Mature Driving, a classroom course developed to refresh your driving skills and in many states help you qualify for lower auto insurance rates

■ Legal Services Network, which assists members in finding prescreened attorneys to help with legal problems

■ Free publications on many subjects relevant to your life

For information: AARP, 601 E St. NW, Washington, DC 20049; 800-424-3410 or 202-434-AARP.

CANADIAN SNOWBIRD ASSOCIATION

CSA is an organization formed to represent the interests of Canadian snowbirds, people who flee the winter snow for the sun and palm trees of the U.S. southern states. As their advocate and lobbying group, CSA addresses issues of concern to Canadian seniors such as health care, absentee voting rights, cross-border problems, residency requirements, U.S. tax laws for Canadians wintering abroad, and estate tax rules on Canadian-owned vacation property in the U.S. And it endorses travel insurance as well as out-of-country health insurance.

Membership costs $10 (single) and $15 (couple) per year, and benefits include a magazine, group travel offerings, an automobile club, a currency-exchange program, mail-order pharmacy services, a discount on membership in AOL, discounts on hotel room rates, and social gatherings in popular snowbird locations such as Florida, Arizona, Texas, and California.

For information: Canadian Snowbird Association, 180 Lesmill Rd., North York, ON M3B 2T5; 800-265-3200 or 416-391-9000.

CARP (CANADIAN ASSOCIATION OF RETIRED PERSONS)

Canadians over the age of 50 are invited to join CARP, a national nonprofit association with about 370,000 members, singles and couples, retired and employed. For a membership fee of $15.95 (Canadian) a year, members get many benefits, including discounted rates on out-of-country health insurance, long-term care insurance, extended health and dental plans, and automobile and home insurance. They can also take advantage of an expanded travel program with discounts on airfares, travel packages, hotels, and car rentals. Members may also participate in the activities of local chapters in their own communities.

CARP publishes a lively, informative, award-winning newspaper called *CARPNews* six times a year, and sponsors national and provincial advocacy programs on issues of major concern to older people, such as pensions, health care, scams, and frauds. Free financial seminars are held frequently throughout the country.

For information: CARP, 27 Queen St. East, Ste. 1304, Toronto, ON M5C 2M6; 800-363-9736 (in Canada) or 416-383-8748.

CATHOLIC GOLDEN AGE

A Catholic nonprofit organization that is concerned with issues affecting older citizens, such as health care, housing, and Social Security benefits, CGA has well over a million members and more than 200 chapters throughout the country. It offers many good things to its members, who must be over 50. These include spiritual benefits, such as masses and prayers worldwide, and practical benefits, such as discounts on hotels, campgrounds, car rentals, and prescriptions. Other offerings include group insurance plans, pilgrimage and group travel programs, and an automobile club. Membership costs $8 a year or $19 for three years.

For information: Catholic Golden Age, 430 Penn Ave., Scranton, PA 18503; 800-836-5699.

GRAY PANTHERS

A national organization of about 20,000 intergenerational activists, the Gray Panthers work on multiple issues that include peace, jobs for all, antidiscrimination (ageism, sexism, racism), family security, the environment, campaign reform, and the United Nations. They are active in more than 50 local networks across the United States in their efforts to promote their goal of advancing social justice. For annual membership dues of $20, members receive a bimonthly newsletter, which is also available by subscription.

For information: Gray Panthers, 733 15th St. NW, Ste. 437, Washington, DC 20005; 800-280-5362 or 202-737-6637.

MEMBERS PRIME CLUB

An association for past or present credit-union employees and volunteers who are at least 50 years old and belong to a credit union, MPC (formerly National Association for Retired Credit Union People, or NARCUP) offers a number of benefits to its members. These include an excellent bimonthly magazine called *Prime Times*; a pharmacy discount program; and discounts on hotels, condominiums, airfares, car and RV rentals, cruises, and vacation packages. Annual membership fee: $49.95.

For information: Members Prime Club, NARCUP, PO Box 391, Madison, WI 53701; 888-889-4373.

NATIONAL ALLIANCE OF SENIOR CITIZENS

This national lobbying organization with over 100,000 members and a decidedly conservative point of view works to influence national policy on key issues such as improving the quality of life for the terminally ill. As a member you receive newsletters and benefits that include group insurance, prescription discounts, discounts on car rentals, lodgings, moving expenses, and an automobile club. Annual dues are $10 for an individual and $15 per family.

For information: National Alliance of Senior Citizens, 1744 Riggs Pl. NW, Washington, DC 20009; 202-986-0117.

NATIONAL ASSOCIATION OF RETIRED FEDERAL EMPLOYEES

As you can probably gather, this is an association of federal retirees and their families. Its primary mission is to protect the earned benefits of retired federal employees via its lobbying program in Washington. Members receive a monthly magazine and are entitled to discounts and special services. *For information:* NARFE, 606 N. Washington St., Alexandria, VA 22314; 800-627-3394 or 703-838-7760.

NATIONAL COUNCIL OF SENIOR CITIZENS

An advocacy organization, NCSC lobbies on the local, state, and national level for legislation benefiting older Americans. With about five million members, it has carried on many campaigns concerning Medicare, housing, health care, Social Security, and other relevant programs.

Although NCSC's major focus is its legislative program, it also has a local club network, social events, prescription discounts, group rates on supplemental health insurance, automobile insurance, and travel discounts, plus a newspaper that keeps you up to date on all of the above. Membership costs $13 a year or $33 for three years.

For information: National Council of Senior Citizens, 8403 Colesville Rd., Ste. 1200, Silver Springs, MD 20910; 800-333-7212 or 301-578-8800.

NATIONAL EDUCATION ASSOCIATION–RETIRED

With a membership of more than 160,000 retired education employees from teachers to school bus drivers,

NEA–Retired acts as an advocate for their special interests such as pensions and health care and supports public education through legislative lobbying as well as reading programs, mentoring, and intergenerational activities. Among its benefits of membership are life, health, disability, and casualty insurance programs; savings and investment plans; credit and loan programs; and discounts, educational guides, and a bimonthly magazine. Join for $15 a year or $100 for life plus local dues that vary by state.

For information: NEA–Retired, 1201 16th St. NW, Washington, DC 20036; 202-822-7149.

OLDER WOMEN'S LEAGUE

OWL is a national nonprofit organization with local chapters dedicated to achieving economic, political, and social equality for older women. Anyone, any age, may join. OWL provides educational materials, training for citizen advocates, and informative publications dealing with the important issues—such as Social Security, health care, retirement benefits, employment discrimination—facing women as they grow older. Annual dues: $25.

For information: Older Women's League, 666 11th St. NW, Washington, DC 20001; 800-825-3695 or 202-783-6686.

THE RETIRED OFFICERS ASSOCIATION

This group is open to anyone who has been a commissioned or warrant officer in the seven U.S. uniformed services. Members receive lobbying representation on Capitol Hill and an excellent magazine that features articles on matters of special interest to them. They may also take advantage of a number of benefits, including discounts on car rentals and motel lodgings, a travel program with "military fares" to many overseas destinations, sports tournaments, a mail-order prescription program, group health and life insurance plans, and a car lease-purchase plan. TROA also has many autonomous local chapters with their own activities and membership fees. Annual dues: $20. Auxiliary members (spouses, widows, or widowers) pay $15 a year.

For information: The Retired Officers Association, 201 N. Washington St., Alexandria, VA 22314; 800-245-8762 or 703-549-2311.

SEARS MATURE OUTLOOK

Sears, the country's largest retailer, has long sponsored Mature Outlook, a discount club for Sears cardholders over the age of 45. But now it offers the program in two varieties: the original Mature Outlook Program and the new Mature Outlook Plus. Both versions offer members discounts on products and services in all Sears stores in the U.S. by giving them money coupons that reduce the prices on regular, sale, and specialty items. It also arranges for discounts on hotels, resorts, restaurants, and car rentals. Annual dues: $19.95 for you and your spouse.

The Plus program greatly enhances the benefits for members by giving them more valuable money coupons, a newsletter, a free car-buying service, and additional money-saving opportunities on such things as airfares, cruises, condos, RV rentals, and prescriptions. Annual dues: $39.95 for you and your spouse.

All members of Mature Outlook receive the bimonthly *Mature Outlook Magazine*, a good read that also keeps you alerted to new savings at Sears.

For information: Mature Outlook, PO Box 9390, Des Moines, IA 50306. Mature Outlook Program: 800-336-6330. Mature Outlook Plus, 800-688-5665.

UNITED SENIORS ASSOCIATION

The United Seniors Association fights for "less government regulation and lower taxes" for seniors. Organized to help stop a national health care plan, its mission is to lobby Congress for its conservative agenda and to get its point of view known via the media, position papers, and a newsletter. Membership costs $5 a year per household.

For information: USA, Inc., 3900 Jermantown Rd., Ste. 450, Fairfax, VA 22030; 800-890-1166 or 703-359-6500.

Index